Sinead Corkett-Beirne

Language and Emotion

A study investigating interjectional usage
by children and adolescents with
Autism Spectrum Disorder, Developmental
Language Disorder, and a
typically developing cohort

Anchor Academic Publishing

Corkett-Beirne, Sinead: Language and Emotion. A study investigating interjectional usage by children and adolescents with Autism Spectrum Disorder, Developmental Language Disorder, and a typically developing cohort, Hamburg, Anchor Academic Publishing 2022

Buch-ISBN: 978-3-96067-226-5
PDF-eBook-ISBN: 978-3-96067-726-0
Druck/Herstellung: Anchor Academic Publishing, Hamburg, 2022

Bibliografische Information der Deutschen Nationalbibliothek:
Die Deutsche Nationalbibliothek verzeichnet diese Publikation in der Deutschen Nationalbibliografie; detaillierte bibliografische Daten sind im Internet über http://dnb.d-nb.de abrufbar.

Bibliographical Information of the German National Library:
The German National Library lists this publication in the German National Bibliography. Detailed bibliographic data can be found at: http://dnb.d-nb.de

© Anchor Academic Publishing, Imprint der Bedey & Thoms Media GmbH
Hermannstal 119k, 22119 Hamburg
https://www.anchor-publishing.com, Hamburg 2022
Printed in Germany

Abstract

Interjections are utterances used to express emotion and they can also be used to convey a speaker's internal mental state. Phatic interjections are used to maintain social communication, which forms part of the triad of impairments in Autism Spectrum Disorder (ASD). Thus far, the study of interjections has been extremely limited in scope. The aim of this preliminary study is to provide an insight into the use of interjections among children and adolescents with ASD, ASD with an accompanying language impairment (ASD-LI), and Developmental Language Disorder (DLD) in comparison to a typically developing (TD) cohort. All participants were asked to generate a story using the picture book *Hug* (Alborough, 2000). Narratives were analysed according to a range of features including the number of propositions, references to frames of mind, and other evaluative devices. Participants also played snakes and ladders, designed to elicit spontaneous language, with the researcher. The number of interjections produced during both tasks was calculated and analysed for type and frequency. While the ASD and TD groups performed on a similar level, the ASD-LI and DLD groups showed notable similarities when they were assessed on their linguistic abilities using the British Picture Vocabulary Scale and the Clinical Evaluation of Language Fundamentals. Groups did not differ in regard to frames of mind references produced during the narrative task or cognitive and emotive interjections during the play session. Furthermore, interjections were produced during character speech by the ASD, ASD-LI and DLD groups. With regard to the number of phatic interjections produced, the ASD and ASD-LI groups did not differ from the TD cohort. The use of interjections by all groups was evident during both the narrative task and play method, with the latter eliciting a broader range. These findings provide a deeper insight into the role of interjections in language and emotion.

Dedication

This book is dedicated to my parents, Angela and Stephen, who have supported me tirelessly throughout my entire life.

Acknowledgements

I am extremely grateful to Dr. Kai Alter and Professor Ghada Khattab for their supervision, support and guidance throughout the duration of my study at Newcastle University. I would also like to extend my appreciation to Dr. Kim Pearce for the time, support, encouragement, and statistical advice she has given me over the past two years. Without her help, I would still be navigating through an Andy Field book to this day.

This research would not have been possible without the incredible support from schools, parents, and teachers. I am eternally grateful for their help in allowing me to conduct this research project. I would like to acknowledge Walbottle Academy, Welbeck Academy, Thomas Bewick School, West Walker Primary School, Tyneview Primary School, and Kenton Primary School for their help in recruiting participants.

Thank you to all the Special Educational Needs Coordinators, speech and language therapists, headteachers, and teachers whom I have engaged with during my time spent working in schools. Also, I am extremely grateful to all the parents who have supported me through allowing me to conduct my research. I wish to proclaim a special thank you to all the children whom I have worked with throughout this project. Without you, this research would not have taken place.

Finally, I would like to thank my family for their continued love, support, and encouragement throughout my entire life. My parents, Angela and Stephen, deserve special recognition. They have always supported me in every decision I make, and I wish to make them proud. Thank you for always being at the receiving end of a phone call and, most importantly, for your words of encouragement which have enabled me to complete this book.

Table of Contents

List of Abbreviations

ADOS-G – Autism Diagnostic Observation Schedule – Generic

ARC – Additionally Resourced Centre

AS – Asperger's Syndrome

ASD – Autism Spectrum Disorder

ASD-LI – Autism Spectrum Disorder with Language Impairment

BNC – British National Corpus

BPVS - British Picture Vocabulary Scale

BPVS-II - British Picture Vocabulary Scale – Second Edition

BPVS-III - British Picture Vocabulary Scale – Third Edition

CELF – Clinical Evaluation of Language Fundamentals

CELF-5 - Clinical Evaluation of Language Fundamentals – Fifth UK Edition

CHILDES – Child Language Data Exchange System

CNTNAP2 – Contactin Associated Protein 2

DLD – Developmental Language Disorder

DSM-5 – Diagnostic and Statistical Manual of Mental Health Disorders (2013)

ELI – Expressive Language Index

fMRI – Functional Magnetic Resonance Imaging

FOXP2 – Forkhead Box Protein P2

ICD-10 – International Classification of Diseases – Tenth Edition (World Health Organization, 2016)

ICD-11 – International Classification of Diseases – Eleventh Edition (World Health Organization, 2018)

LARSP - Language Assessment, Remediation and Screening Procedure

LCI – Language Content Index

MRI – Magnetic Resonance Imaging

RLI – Receptive Language Index

SENTASS – Special Educational Needs Teaching and Support Service

SLI – Specific Language Impairment

TD – Typical Development

List of Figures

List of Tables

Chapter 1. Introduction

Autism Spectrum Disorder and Developmental Language Disorder are two distinct neuro-developmental disorders whereby the onset of symptoms is present during the initial stages of a person's life (American Psychiatric Association, 2013). In England, the estimated prevalence of Autism Spectrum Disorder (ASD) is 1.1 per cent (Brugha *et al.*, 2012, p. 28). Like ASD, Developmental Language Disorder (DLD) is a common neurodevelopmental disorder. With an estimated prevalence of 7.58 per cent, approximately two out of thirty children in a classroom will have a clinically significant language disorder whereby the cause remains unknown (Norbury *et al.* 2016, p. 1253). Despite being almost seven times more common than ASD, Developmental Language Disorder is under-studied (McGregor, 2020).

1.1   Description and Diagnostic Criteria for Autism Spectrum Disorder

There are a triad of impairments that form the criteria for a diagnosis of Autism Spectrum Disorder (ASD) including persistent deficits in social communication, social interaction, and restricted, repetitive patterns of behaviour (American Psychiatric Association, 2013). The Diagnostic and Statistical Manual of Mental Health Disorders – Fifth Edition (DSM-5, American Psychiatric Association, 2016) is used by clinicians and psychiatrists and, according to the updated version, an individual must present with all of the following communicative deficits to receive a diagnosis for ASD: social and emotional exchanges, non-verbal methods of communication, and deficits in the ability to develop, maintain, and understand rela-tionships. Individuals with ASD tend to show less interest in engaging with others and initiating interactions. Although some individuals with ASD are able to deliver an extensive monologue about a subject that interests them, difficulties lay in turn-taking and being able to hold a conversation about the same topic between two or more people. Non-verbal behaviours are also a difficulty for individuals with ASD as they may avoid making eye contact, struggle to decode facial expressions, and they may avoid using gestures.

The level of severity in ASD is wide-ranging as each person's profile is individualistic, differing from another person diagnosed with the same pervasive neurodevelopmental disorder (Kjelgaard and Tager Flusberg, 2001; Lord *et al.*, 2018). According to the DSM-5 (American Psychiatric Association, 2013), severity levels for ASD can be divided into three categories according to social communication and restricted, repetitive behaviours. The first level identifies the individual as requiring support; the second level requires substantial support, and the third level requires very substantial support. There are several factors which may influence this including a person's chronological age, their intellectual functioning, and language abilities (American Psychiatric Association, 2013). In the DSM-5 (American Psychiatric Association, 2013), Autistic Disorder, Childhood Disintegrative Disorder, Pervasive Developmental Disorder – Not Otherwise Specified, and Asperger Syndrome have been merged into one umbrella term, Autism Spectrum Disorder, to provide a more accurate diagnosis. Prior to this, the four disorders were treated as separate diagnoses. Asperger Syndrome, for example, was diagnosed if an individual had an IQ of 70 or above and no language delay was reported during childhood. Overall, there is a tendency for researchers to recruit individuals with ASD whose language abilities are classed as being within the normal range. Considering that at least half of all children with ASD have intellectual disabilities, a large proportion of the ASD population is omitted from research (Mody and Belliveau, 2013, p. 158).

1.2 Description and Diagnostic Criteria for Language Disorder

There are different modes of language including the spoken, written, and signed form. Also categorised as a communication disorder in the DSM-5 (American Psychiatric Association, 2013), the diagnostic criteria for Language Disorder includes persistent difficulties in the acquisition and use of language. This is a result of comprehension and/or production deficits including reduced vocabulary, limited sentence structures, and impairments in discourse (American Psychiatric Association, 2013). Structural language includes grammar and phonology; these aspects are limited in children with a language disorder. Thus, poor sentence repetition and the repetition of non-words are a clinical marker of the disorder (Tomblin, 2011).

Language Disorder is heterogeneous as each person has their own idiolect and severity differs among individuals (Tager-Flusberg, 2015, p. 1045). Standardised language assessments are often administered to individuals susceptible of having a Language Disorder. Diagnostic criteria for a language impairment involve language achievement levels below cut-off values of 1.0 to 1.5 standard deviations below age expectations. If a person's performance during these tests reaches two standard deviations below the mean, the results are indicative of a severe language disorder (Kjelgaard and Tager-Flusberg, 2001). A moderate language disorder is diagnosed if assessment results reach 1.5 standard deviations below the mean. There is variation in which standard deviation score is used within previous research studies. It is therefore worth bearing in mind the severity of language disorder among participants when collating results from previous studies and using the findings in conjunction with one-another.

Until recently, the term Specific Language Impairment (SLI) was widely used to refer to children whose language abilities are significantly below age expectations when compared to their typically developing peers (Bishop *et al.*, 2017). The DSM-5 (American Psychiatric Association, 2013), however, excludes the term Specific Language Impairment whereas Language Disorder is used to refer to the condition instead. To clarify, Language Disorder and language impairment are terms that can be used interchangeably to refer to an individual presenting with comprehension and/or production deficits. Within the past few years, interest has been generated addressing the suitability of the term SLI and its appropriateness for use. An alternative proposal to SLI was suggested following a review meeting consisting of speech and language therapists, psychologists, paediatricians, psychiatrists, specialist teachers, and charity representatives. One outcome of the meeting proposed distinguishing between Language Disorder associated with a biomedical condition and Developmental Language Disorder (DLD), whereby an individual has language difficulties which are not associated with a known biomedical condition (Bishop *et al.*, 2017). It is important to make the distinction between the two as the term Language Disorder, used in the DSM-5 (American Psychiatric Association, 2013), encompasses both Developmental Language Disorder and Language Disorder associated with a biomedical condition. This is outlined in Table 1. In England, the prevalence of Language Impairment associated with existing medical diagnoses and/or intellectual disorder is 2.34 per cent whereas 7.58 per cent of the population is estimated to have a clinically significant language disorder whereby the cause is unknown (Norbury *et al.*, 2016, p. 1253). The latter is referred to as Developmental Language Disorder and, from this point forward, the term will be used where appropriate. Also, the term Specific Language Impairment will be used throughout this book in reference to previous research studies whereby this was the name used at the time of publication.

Terminology	Definition
Language Disorder	The term provided in the DSM-5 which is used in reference to language difficulties as a result of comprehension and/or production deficits. Language Disorder encompasses Developmental Language Disorder and Language Disorder associated with a biomedical condition.
Specific Language Impairment	The term used to refer to children who present with selective language difficulties whereby the cause is unknown.
Language Disorder associated with a biomedical condition	The term provided when language disorder is part of a more complex pattern of impairments. Biomedical conditions can include Autism Spectrum Disorder, intellectual disabilities, hearing impairment, cerebral palsy, neurodegenerative conditions, and genetic conditions such as Downs Syndrome.
Developmental Language Disorder	The term given when language disorder does not occur with another biomedical condition. Language difficulties may include phonology, syntax and morphology, semantics, word finding, pragmatics, and verbal learning and memory.

Table 1.   A table containing terminology and definitions (Royal College of Speech and Language Therapists, 2017)

1.2.1   Exclusionary Criteria for a Diagnosis of Developmental Language Disorder

There are a number of criteria which a person must meet to obtain a diagnosis of Developmental Language Disorder, formerly referred to as SLI. For example, an individual must not have a co-occurring neurological disorder (Bartlett *et al.*, 2012). Children with SLI must not have any developmental or sensory impairments; thus, they must not have problems with their hearing, non-verbal intelligence, motor skills, and social and affective status (Tomblin, 1996). ASD is also a part of the exclusionary criteria as children with SLI cannot present with the restricted, repetitive patterns of behaviour characteristic of autism (Tomblin, 2011).

1.3   Similarities between Autism Spectrum Disorder and Developmental Language Disorder

Autism Spectrum Disorder and Developmental Language Disorder are two distinct neuro-developmental disorders although they tend to commonly co-occur with one another which is indicative of a shared aetiology (Bishop, 2010). The aetiologies of ASD and DLD are unknown although previous studies have reported influences in genetic predisposition. Interestingly, the DSM-5 (American Psychiatric Association, 2013) classifies Language Disorder as a commu-nication disorder. Similarly, social communication forms part of the triad of impairments in ASD. Thus, poor spoken communication skills are a common feature in children with SLI and ASD (Tomblin, 2011). While structural aspects of language are limited in SLI, this is extremely variable in ASD. Some children with ASD are non-verbal whereas others have poor language skills. Also, some children with ASD have an extensive vocabulary and their phonological and grammatical skills are intact (Tomblin, 2011). Discrepancies in the linguistic profiles of ASD and SLI have been used to argue that the two disorders are independent from one another. ASD, therefore, does not exclude SLI as an individual with ASD can have an accompanying language impairment. This overlap indicates that the two disorders are co-morbid, defined as the oc-currence of two or more diseases in one individual, and hereby related to one another. It must be noted, however, that the DSM-5 (American Psychiatric Association, 2013) does not discuss Autism Spectrum Disorder with an accompanying language impairment.

Similarities in the linguistic, neurological, and genetic profiles of SLI and ASD have been reported. Language impairment is commonplace in ASD, and this clinical population is re-ferred to as ASD-LI in previous literature (Williams *et al.*, 2008). For example, Tager-Flusberg and Joseph (2003, p. 304) found that 47 per cent of children with autism had a severe language impairment in their study and the language abilities of 30 per cent of autistic children were bordering on impaired. In a separate study, Tager-Flusberg and Joseph (2003) used Magnetic Resonance Imaging (MRI) scans to investigate neurological features in ASD and typical development. There were 16 boys with autism who partook in the study, all of whom had nor-mal non-verbal intelligent quotient (IQ) scores, and 15 typically developing boys matched according to age and handedness. Broca's area is a region of the brain situated in the inferior lateral frontal cortex and it is composed of two regions: pars opercularis and pars triangularis. The production of language is associated with Broca's area (Temple, 1993). MRI scans detected that the pars opercularis region of Broca's area was 27 per cent larger in the right hemisphere in the boys with autism whereas this region was 17 per cent larger in the left hemisphere in the typically developing boys (Tager-Flusberg and Joseph, 2003, p. 306). No other notable differences were detected. Interestingly, the reversed asymmetry detected in the boys with autism is similar to findings reported in SLI. Gauger *et al.* (1997), for example, found that the pars triangularis region of Broca's area was significantly smaller in children with SLI compared to typically developing children. Also, the children with SLI were more likely than the typically developing children to have a rightward asymmetry of the pars triangularis and planum temporale (Gauger *et al.*, 1997). Similarly, a study conducted by De Fossé *et al.* (2004) found that children with autism and normal language skills and typically developing children had similar leftward volumetric asymmetry of the inferior frontal gyrus, pars opercularis and pars triangularis. It must be noted that 'the asymmetry of the inferior frontal gyrus correlated with verbal intelligent quotient scores, but not with non-verbal IQ scores, which further supports the relationship between Broca's area asymmetry and language abilities in right-handed subjects' (De Fossé *et al.*, 2004, p. 762). Meanwhile, the children with autism and an accompanying language impairment and children with Specific Language Impairment had reversed rightward asymmetry in the inferior frontal gyrus (De Fossé *et al.*, 2004). Also, the children with autism and an accompanying language impairment and the children with Specific Language Impairment had significant asymmetry of the planum temporale. This finding was not reported for the children with autism and normal language skills and the typically developing children. Consequently, the study can be used to support the claim that there is an association between language diagnosis and prominent leftward asymmetry of the planum temporale (De Fossé *et al.*, 2004, p. 763). One notable finding from the study was that the children with autism and a language impairment shared similar neurological profiles to the children with SLI, demonstrated through both groups having reversal frontal language asymmetry (De Fossé *et al.*, 2004). These results can provide further support to the claim that there is a common neurobiological basis of language impairment in ASD and SLI (De Fossé *et al.*, 2004). Although it has gained traction, further research into the neurobiology underpinning language impairment in ASD and DLD is warranted to gain an understanding of the co-morbidities.

Genetic studies have detected there is a higher rate of autism in the siblings of individuals with SLI (Tomblin *et al.*, 2003; Pickles *et al.*, 2013). Twin studies are often used to determine the influence of genetics. Monozygotic twins are genetically identical whereas dizygotic twins share approximately 50 per cent of their genes (Leonard, 2014, p. 188). Thus, if monozygotic twins are more concordant than dizygotic twins then there is evidence for a genetic influence on disorder (Bishop, 2009). Folstein and Rutter (1977, p. 727) reported that four out of the eleven monozygotic twins included in their study were concordant for autism, whereas this was not detected in the dizygotic twins. Interestingly, the majority of the monozygotic twins had some form of cognitive disorder, including a speech or language impairment, whereas this was not as prevalent in the dizygotic twins (Folstein and Rutter, 1977). This is exemplified through 82 per cent of the monozygotic twins being concordant for some form of cognitive disorder whereas this was 10 per cent for the dizygotic twins (Folstein and Rutter, 1977, p. 727). A follow-up study conducted by Bailey *et al.* (1995) provided additional support for these results. With regard to molecular genetics, there is a reported association between common forms of language impairment, such as non-word repetition which is a clinical marker of the disorder, and variants of the gene Contactin Associated Protein 2 (CNTNAP2) which is regulated by Forkhead box protein P2 (FOXP2) (Vernes *et al.*, 2008). The genetic code is contained within the nucleus of a cell body, which is a part of a neuron. One region of significant interest is the intronic single nucleotide polymorphism (SNP) rs2710102 in the CNTNAP2 gene as it associated with non-word repetition and language impairment (Vernes *et al.*, 2008), as well as a delayed onset of speech in ASD measured by the age in which a child produces their first word (Alarcón *et al.*, 2008). It should be noted that the CNTNAP2 gene was restricted to the frontal and anterior temporal lobes, striatum, and dorsal thalamus (Alarcón *et al.*, 2008, p. 150). This study indicates that genetics is a determining factor in language impairment in autism as the developmental expression of the CNTNAP2 gene influenced brain circuitry effected in ASD (Alarcón *et al.*, 2008, p. 157).

1.4 Overview of Interjections

Interjections are defined as linguistic expressions used to express emotion and they can also be used to convey the attitude or mental state of a speaker (Fraser, 1990; Ameka, 1992; Wierzbicka, 1992; Metcalfe *et al.*, 2009; Wharton, 2009; Stange, 2016; Downing and Martínez Caro, 2019). As well as expressing emotions, interjections can be used to fulfil a range of different functions including expressing a person's knowledge, requesting attention, greeting people, and bidding farewell to them (Clark and Fox Tree, 2002). Interjections can be sub-divided into several different categories including the cognitive, emotive, phatic, and volitive (Wierzbicka, 1992; Goddard, 2014). Cognitive interjections convey information states and the knowledge of a person which tend to be related to the time in which an utterance is spoken (Ameka, 1992; Goddard, 2014). Emotive interjections are used to convey the emotions and sensations that a speaker experiences at a given time; examples include *yuck*, *wow*, *ouch*, and *ugh* (Ameka, 1992). Phatic interjections play an important role during social interactions as they can be used to maintain social and communicative contact between a speaker and listener (Ameka, 1992). Examples of phatic interjections include the discourse markers *uh-huh* or *mm* and they are often used by a listener to indicate that they are paying attention to a speaker's utterance during spoken discourse. Volitive interjections are used to convey a person wanting something in the semantic meaning of their utterance; an example of this would be the English interjection *ssh!* (Wierzbicka, 1992; Goddard, 2014).

1.5   Research Aims

The present research has two aims. The first aim of this study is to identify similarities and differences in the linguistic abilities of children and adolescents with Autism Spectrum Disorder (ASD), Autism Spectrum Disorder with an accompanying language impairment (ASD-LI), Developmental Language Disorder (DLD), and a typically developing (TD) cohort. The second aim is in fact the focal point of this study, and this involves investigating inter-jectional usage by children and adolescents with ASD, ASD-LI, DLD, and a TD cohort.

1.6   Structure of the book

This book comprises ten chapters. The preliminary section, Chapter 1, introduces Autism Spectrum Disorder and Developmental Language Disorder. As previously stated, interjections are the central focus of investigation in this study therefore they are introduced in the first chapter. An overview of the human nervous system is discussed in Chapter 2 and an insight into the neurobiological underpinnings of language is provided. Chapter 3 explores emotion recognition and expression, and the relationship between language and emotion is also dis-cussed. An understanding of their interrelation is important as interjections are defined as ut-terances which typically express emotion. Chapter 4 provides an overview of the acquisition of language and the rules which underpin it. Pragmatic abilities and theory of mind in relation to ASD and DLD is also addressed in this section. Chapter 5 centres on narratives, and comparisons are drawn between individuals with ASD, DLD, and a typically developing cohort in regard to their linguistic and narrative abilities. Chapter 6 explores previous literature on the topic of interjections. The methodological procedures used for the current study are discussed in Chapter 7 and participation selection is addressed. The results of the study are provided in Chapter 8 which is subsequently followed by a discussion of the findings in Chapter 9. Finally, Chapter 10 concludes the findings of the current study and suggestions for future research topics are provided.

Chapter 2. The Human Nervous System

The anatomy of a human being consists of a central nervous system and the peripheral nervous system. The central nervous system consists of the brain and the spinal cord which are connected through the brain stem. The peripheral system extends from the brain to regions throughout the human body; nerve cells transmit signals between these, providing information about movement and balance, pain, pressure, and the five basic senses: touch, vision, hearing, smell, and taste (Baars and Gage, 2018). There are twelve cranial nerves contained within the peripheral nervous system, each of which has their own individual function such as controlling eye movements, vocalisations, facial expressions, chewing, respiration, heart rate, and digestion (Ten Donkelaar *et al.*, 2011).

The basic unit of the nervous system consists of a neuron which is physiologically composed of the soma, dendrites, and an axon as demonstrated in Figure 1.

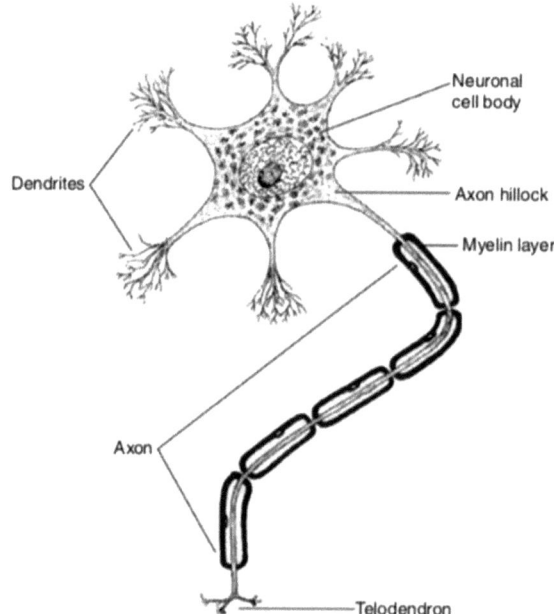

Figure 1. The structure of a neuron (Augustine 2017, p. 2)

A neuron and a nerve cell are terms that can be used interchangeably. The soma, also called the cell body, contains the nucleus which is where genetic material is stored including chromosomes formed from deoxyribonucleic acid (DNA) (Noback *et al.*, 2005). Neurons are cells which receive, process, and store information. Dendrites receive information from other cells whereas the axon transmits information to other neurons (Ward, 2015). Although a neuron has one axon, it can have several branches of dendrites. The terminal of an axon transmits chemical signals to the dendrite of another neuron through a small gap situated between the neurons, referred to as a synapse (Ward, 2015). These chemical signals are called neurotransmitters.

2.1 The Central Nervous System

The brain and spinal cord, also known as the central nervous system, contains neurons which are organised to form white matter and grey matter. White matter consists of axons and glial cells which support neurons. The axons located in the white matter of the spinal cord transmit signals from this region to higher parts of the central nervous system (Brodal, 2004). Grey matter consists of nerve cell bodies and axons are transmitted from the central nervous system to other regions of the human body via the spinal cord (Brodal, 2004).

The human brain consists of three parts: the brainstem, cerebellum, and cerebrum. The cerebrum is divided into two cerebral hemispheres: the left and right. The cerebral hemispheres contain a central cavity, referred to as the lateral ventricle, which is surrounded by white matter (Brodal, 2004). The cerebral cortex is the outer layer of the brain, which forms the surface of the two cerebral hemispheres, and it is composed of grey matter (Baars and Gage, 2018). Most human cognition occurs in the cerebral cortex; this includes internal cognitive processes such as planning and decision making (Baars and Gage, 2018). Visual, auditory, somatosensory, smell, and taste inputs are all senses processed in the cerebral cortex (Baars and Gage, 2018). The left and right cerebral hemispheres are separate from one another although they are connected through the corpus callosum, composed of white matter, which transmits information between the two hemispheres (Brodal, 2004). Each cerebral hemisphere contains primary sensory areas which are regions specialised in processing sensory information from the eyes, ears, and other regions of the body (Baars and Gage, 2018). These are known as the primary visual cortex, primary auditory cortex, and the primary somatosensory cortex. Each cerebral hemisphere is composed of four cortical lobes: frontal, parietal, temporal, and occipital. This is demonstrated in Figure 2. The four cortical lobes are all part of the cerebral cortex and they serve different functions in human cognition (Baars and Gage 2018, p. 22).

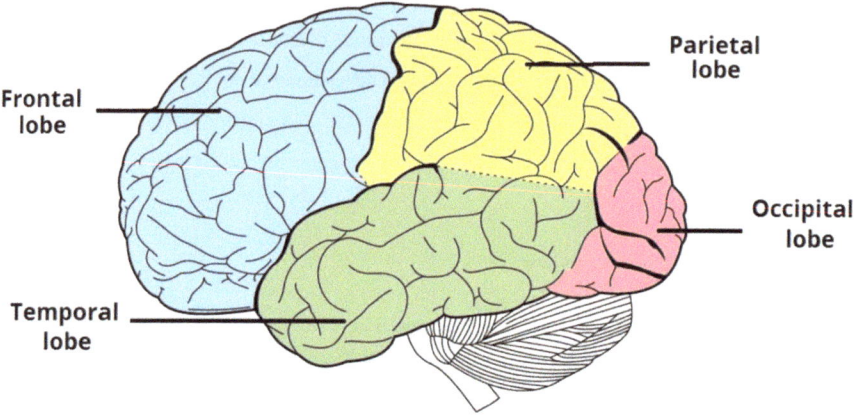

Figure 2. The lobes of the cerebral cortex (Irshad, 2018)

The frontal lobe is home to the motor cortex which controls the planning and execution of movement and actions. Different regions of the motor cortex have control over different parts of the human body (Baars and Gage, 2018). The prefrontal cortex is situated in the front region of the frontal lobe and it is an area of interest as it controls a wide range of executive functions; the latter term refers to a set of cognitive processes and they play an important role during everyday life. Decision making, focusing one's attention, planning, and setting goals are some examples of executive functions (Baars and Gage, 2018). In addition to this, perspective-taking, problem solving, and reasoning are cognitive functions controlled by the prefrontal cortex (Clark *et al.*, 2018). There are a number of impairments characteristic of ASD which indicates a dysfunction of the prefrontal cortex (Clark *et al.*, 2018). For example, executive functions play a fundamental role during social interactions as humans form perceptions about the behaviour of others and their interpretations can influence the response they provide. The CNTNAP2 gene is expressed in the prefrontal cortex and genetic variants have been associated with autism and language impairment (Alarcon *et al.*, 2008). There are several regions contained within the prefrontal cortex, each fulfilling their own function. The left ventrolateral prefrontal cortex, for example, is specialised in processing language and producing speech (Clark *et al.*, 2018). This specific region of the brain encompasses Broca's area, composed of pars opercularis and pars triangularis, which controls the production of language. Broca's area is therefore activated during the retrieval and generation of words. Broca's area is situated next to the motor cortex, although it is worth highlighting that the premotor cortex interconnects with Broca's area as neurons transmit information to the facial region of the primary motor cortex which controls the muscles required for speech production and writing (Clark *et al.*, 2018). The right ventrolateral prefrontal cortex controls the patterns of stress and intonation in a language, known as prosody (Clark *et al.*, 2018).

The parietal lobes are primarily responsible for processing sensory information from the muscles and skin including touch, temperature, pressure, and pain. The occipital lobe is the visual processing area of the brain therefore it is home to the primary visual cortex. This region of the brain is responsible for sight as well as the recognition and perception of images. The temporal lobe can be divided into two regions: dorsolateral and ventromedial. The dorsolateral region provides support to cognitive functions which are associated with sensory systems, including language (Clark *et al.*, 2018). The ventromedial region of the temporal lobe contributes to emotional tone. The temporal lobe contains the primary auditory cortex and neurons in this region of the brain are responsive to sounds. The superior temporal gyrus plays a fundamental part in auditory perception and speech (Clark *et al.*, 2018). For example, the left inferior temporal gyrus processes word sounds, and the middle temporal gyrus processes semantic information as it matches word sounds with meanings (Clark *et al.*, 2018). Wernicke's area, located in the posterior region of the superior temporal gyrus, controls the perception of speech (Clark *et al.*, 2018). Wernicke's area is situated next to the primary auditory cortex. Language is complex and a range of cognitive skills are required to process information such as memorising, learning, reasoning, and attentional skills (Sperber and Wilson, 1992). Language is a neurobiological function, and the production of speech is primarily associated with the left hemisphere of the brain. Nevertheless, the ability to identify voices and emotional content through prosody is associated with the right cerebral hemisphere (Clark *et al.*, 2018). The right hemisphere also plays a minor linguistic role as it allows for the comprehension of non-literal language such as sarcasm, irony, and metaphors (Temple 1993, p. 98). These are linguistic difficulties associated with ASD. Thus, it can be suggested that a language impairment may be influenced by the neurological functioning of Broca and/or Wernicke's area as a diagnosis is based on a person exhibiting production and/or comprehension deficits.

Chapter 3. Language and Emotion

Emotions are defined as a mental state or feeling which occur in response to a person's circumstances, their mood, or their relationship with others (Oxford English Dictionary, 2011). According to the basic theory of emotion, there are six universal states: anger, disgust, enjoyment, fear, sadness, and surprise (Ekman, no date). Emotions are an important part of everyday life as a person may experience some of the basic emotions on a daily basis (Ekman, 1992). Consequently, the six universal states previously listed often feature within emotion research. Humans, however, are incredibly complex beings and the emotions that we feel are not restricted to the six states listed under the basic emotion theory. More complex states such as guilt, shame, and disappointment are not accounted for under the basic theory of emotion. A more exhaustive list of emotional states is presented in Figure 3.

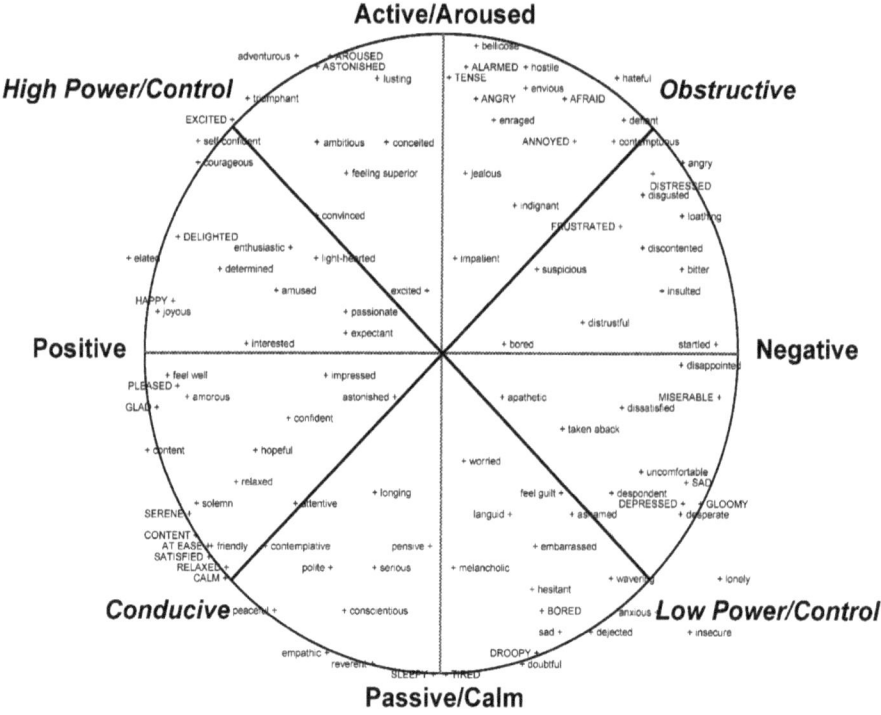

Figure 3. Alternative dimensional structures of the semantic space for emotions (Scherer, 2005, p. 720)

The onset of emotions can be rapid and often there is great variation in the duration of their length. Some people may experience emotions which are brief whereas other emotions are long-lasting (Ekman, 1992; Ekman and Cordaro, 2011). Surprise, for example, is classed as the briefest emotion as it is triggered by a sudden and unexpected onset (Ekman and Friesen, 2003). Emotions are often elicited by events as personal experiences can trigger a response. The behaviour and actions of other people, for example, can influence a person's emotions (Scherer, 2005). Thus, it is worth noting that both external and internal events can elicit emotions. Memories are stored across different regions of the brain which are interconnected. The cognitive process of recalling an event a person experienced during their lifetime is an example of how internal events can influence our emotions. Pride, guilt, and shame are emotions often experienced by a person reflecting on their own behaviour (Scherer, 2005). Also, it is worth noting that emotions can occur in response to a stimulus which is present or imaginary.

Considering that feelings are subjective, the most accurate and appropriate method of identifying the emotions a person experiences would be to invite them to report on it first-hand (Scherer, 2005). Nevertheless, Scherer (1986) highlights that asking a person to reveal their emotional state does not necessarily guarantee a truthful answer will be provided. There are two dominant approaches that psychologists have used to measure self-reported emotional experiences to date: the discrete emotions method and the dimensional approach (Scherer, 2005). Firstly, emotion words form the basis of categorisation in the discrete approach. Emotion words must encapsulate the affiliated facial and vocal expressions and physiological changes (Scherer, 2005). Fear, for example, is defined as pain or uneasiness which arises when there is a sense of impending danger or the prospect of harm (Oxford English Dictionary, 2021). Facial expressions depicting fear include raised eyebrows and upper eyelids, tensed lower eyelids, lowering of the jaw, and lips stretched backwards (Ekman, no date). Also, vocal expressions associated with fear include a higher pitch and strained tone and, in some cases, a person may omit a scream (Ekman, no date). Language therefore plays a pivotal role in distinguishing the different emotional states from one-another. Second, the dimensional approach postulates that emotions can be posited in a three-dimensional space based upon the dimensions of valence (positive-negative), arousal (calm-excited), and tension (tense-relaxed) (Scherer, 2005, p. 718). This is demonstrated in Figure 3.

Emotions can be expressed non-verbally through facial expressions, gestures, and body language as well as through the use of vocalisations (Asano, 1997). The human face is the focal point in expressing and communicating emotion, thus the vast majority of emotion recognition studies have centred upon this. With this in mind, the ability to accurately form an interpretation about another person's internal state based upon their facial expressions alone can aid successful communication during social interactions (Tseng *et al.*, 2014). Facial expressions, however, can be manipulated. For example, a person may conceal their internal sad emotional state by making a conscious effort to smile. This portrayal is often used to deceive other people into thinking that they feel happy (Yield *et al.*, 2012). Taking this into consideration, it can be suggested that facial expressions are not an entirely representative way of gaining an insight into a person's state of mind. In the same vein, individuals may utter verbal expressions whereby the literal, semantic meaning is contrary to how they are feeling internally. For example, a person may utter *I'm fine* after receiving upsetting information which they are trying to process, and they may wish to do so alone. The tone of voice in which utterances are spoken can indicate a speaker's affective state, hereby reinforcing Darwin's (1872) claim that the vocal organs are in fact the most efficient means of expression in both mankind and animals. This claim can be reinforced through highlighting that human beings are exposed to sounds in their environment and they constantly receive auditory signals whereas eye gaze can be averted. Tone of voice, however, is a perceptual feature and listeners must be able to take a range of factors into account to formulate inferences about speaker's true emotional states to allow for successful communication.

The study of non-verbal aspects of emotions has been the primary focus in research to date whereas language used to express emotion warrants further investigation (Scherer, 1986; Keltner and Ekman, 2003; Goddard, 2014). Non-verbal and verbal methods of emotional expression can work in conjunction with one-another as some vocalisations may be accompanied by facial expressions and gestures. For example, a person may utter *ouch* to express their pain while simultaneously closing their eyes and wrinkling their nose. The use of language to express emotions can be measured in a number of different ways including assessing a person's ability to comprehend words conveying a range of emotions, discussing emotions, and investigating the perception and production of emotional intonation in speech (Lartseva, 2015, p. 2).

The recognition and expression of emotions are often treated as separate entities and they are rarely studied in conjunction with one-another (Bänziger *et al.*, 2015). Emotional recognition has been studied much more extensively than emotional expression therefore further research into the latter is warranted (Yiend *et al.*, 2012; Bänziger *et al.*, 2015). Emotion recognition involves forming an interpretation about another person's emotional state and it can play a significant role during social interactions as interlocutors may express how they are feeling to other people (Hepach *et al.*, 2011). The receiver may respond by communicating their own thoughts and feelings; by doing so, the reciprocation of such information can lead to the establishment, development, and sustainability of some relationships. Thus, the ability to identify and comprehend emotions as well as attribute emotional states to other people is a fundamental part of communication as it allows for the formulation of inferences about another person's mental state which can explain their behaviour and actions. The format for most emotion recognition studies involve showing photographic images or videos to participants, each containing an emotion visibly depicted on the facial expressions included. Participants are then instructed to match the emotional expression with a verbal label, other facial images, or a corresponding vocal expression. There are some disadvantages of using standardised lists of emotion labels. For example, participants are restricted to a selection of emotion labels to choose from and they may have selected an emotion which is not included, provided they were given the freedom to choose (Scherer, 2005). Also, participants must be familiar with the emotion labels to ensure accuracy.

3.1   Emotion Recognition in Autism Spectrum Disorder

While it is accepted that individuals with ASD have emotion recognition deficits, prior studies have presented conflicted findings. On the one hand, studies have reported that children with ASD are as capable as typically developing individuals at recognising basic emotions (Castelli, 2005). Castelli's (2005) study found that children with autism or Asperger's Syndrome (AS) are as capable as typically developing children at recognising facial expressions depicting the six basic emotions. The study involved assessing participants abilities to match standardised photographic images of facial expressions, depicting various emotions at different intensity levels, to an appropriate emotion label. The emotions consisted of happiness, anger, surprise, disgust, fear, and sadness. It is worth noting that the vast majority of studies investigating emotion recognition using individuals with ASD have focused on the six basic emotions. Thus, future research studies should incorporate simple emotions alongside more complex states to determine performance abilities during emotion recognition tasks. Referring back to Castelli's (2005) study, there are some limitations which must be considered. Firstly, two different assessments were used to calculate the verbal mental ages of the children with autism and the control group. Thus, the methodological procedures used in the study are not consistent. This can be exemplified through the children with autism or Asperger Syndrome being administered the Wechsler Intelligence Scale for Children – Third Edition (1992), eliciting verbal intelligent quotient (IQ) and performance IQ scores. By contrast, the control group consisted of typically developing children whose scores were obtained using the British Picture Vocabulary Scale – Second Edition (BPVS-II, 1997). The study may have been more insightful if more complex emotions were included as emotion recognition deficits seem to be more apparent when high-functioning individuals with ASD are assessed on their ability to recognise more complex emotions (Heaton et al., 2012).

On the other hand, studies have found that children with ASD do not perform as well as their typically developing peers during emotion recognition tasks (Losh and Capps, 2003; Loukusa et al., 2014; Taylor et al., 2015). Emotional understanding was explored in Losh and Capps' (2003) study, and they reported that children with autism or Asperger's syndrome (AS) performed significantly worse than their typically developing peers during tasks. This was measured through participants being assessed on their ability to provide appropriate definitions for a range of simple, complex, and complex, self-conscious emotions. In addition to this, participants were assessed on their emotional understanding abilities through having to match emotion words to a series of video clips depicting the following emotions: happiness, fear, anger, shame, and sadness. Adults with ASD have also been found to perform significantly worse compared to a typically developing cohort when they were assessed on their ability to match non-verbal and verbal vocalisations expressing six basic emotions to an appropriate emotion word (Heaton et al., 2012). Examples of non-verbal vocalisations included were laughing, used to express happiness, and crying sounds which depict sadness. Interestingly, the severity of symptoms of alexithymia was strongly associated with the recognition of external emotion cues in individuals with ASD (Heaton et al., 2012, p. 2547). Alexithymia is a term used to refer to the difficulties a person has in being able to identify and describe their feelings and emotional states as well as communicate these to other people (Ricciardi et al., 2015; Poquérusse et al., 2018). Difficulties in being able to distinguish between feelings and bodily sensations of emotional arousal are also a feature associated with alexithymia (Taylor et al., 1991), as well as externally orientated thinking and a limited imaginative capacity (Ricciardi *et al.*, 2015). There is a high prevalence of alexithymia co-occurring with ASD as it has been estimated that half the number of individuals diagnosed with ASD also have alexithymia (Poquérusse *et al.*, 2018, p. 1196). Narrative styles have also been found to be impoverished in individuals with alexithymia, most notably in the ability to use figurative language and metaphors (Poquérusse *et al.*, 2018). Similarly, prior studies have found that children with ASD have difficulty in understanding figurative language (MacKay and Shaw, 2004). To clarify, figurative language is defined as the use of words which deviate from the literal, semantic meaning to convey a message. Some examples of figurative language include similes, metaphors, idioms, hyperbole, and onomatopoeia. *It's raining cats and dogs* is an idiom used to describe extremely heavy rainfall, and the listener must be familiar with this meaning to arrive at the correct interpretation of a speaker's utterance.

3.2 Emotion Recognition in Specific Language Impairment

A study conducted by Merkenschlager *et al.* (2012) found that children with Expressive Specific Language Impairment performed significantly worse than typically developing children when they were assessed on their person and emotion recognition abilities. Criteria for Expressive Specific Language Impairment consisted of children's language skills being two standard deviations below chronological age expectations and one standard deviation discrepancy between language skill and non-verbal intelligence. The person recognition task involved presenting children with slides containing actors and actresses whom they had to identify while watching a scene from a film. The emotion recognition task contained several components: choosing one of five stationary images from a scene in a film, choosing a line drawing matching a corresponding emotional expression, and conveying the emotional content in the scene through either providing a verbal description or re-enacting it. Joy, fear, anger, and pain were the emotions studied as they are representative of everyday life situations (Merkenschlager *et al.*, 2012). One limitation of the study is that Merkenschlager *et al.* (2012) did not make a distinction between the different emotional states and performance, therefore it cannot be deciphered whether the children with Expressive Language Impairment had difficulty recognising all emotional states or whether it was specific to positive or negative valence.

Ford and Milosky (2003) found that children with Language Impairment are more likely to infer emotions of a different valence compared to typically developing children; an example of this would be mistaking mad for a facial expression depicting happiness. Four emotions were investigated in this study: happy, surprised, mad, and sad. While every child in the Language Impaired group produced valence errors, this was not the case for the typically developing group. During the inferencing task, children listened to a story and they were then asked to select a line-drawn facial expression corresponding to how the main character is feeling. Misinterpreting emotions of a different valence can have a negative impact during social interactions as it may lead to a person providing an inappropriate response (Ford and Milosky, 2003). Children with Language Impairment, however, were as proficient as their typically developing peers during an emotion labelling task; this involved the presentation of line-drawn facial expressions and children then had to identify which image depicted happiness, surprise, mad, and sad emotions. Interestingly, one child with Language Impairment labelled a picture expressing surprise as *Oh my!* It is worth highlighting that *oh my* is an interjection used to express surprise or admiration (Oxford English Dictionary, 2021). Children with Language Impairment also performed as well as their typically developing peers during the emotion comprehension task, which involved pointing to a drawing of a corresponding facial expression upon hearing the emotion label. Together, these findings indicate that children with Language Impairment are as proficient as their typically developing peers at identifying and compre-hending basic emotions, however their difficulties lay in inferring emotions in contextual circumstances.

3.3 Emotion Recognition in Autism Spectrum Disorder and Specific Language Impairment

The number of studies investigating possible overlaps of socio-cognitive characteristics, such as emotion recognition, in Autism Spectrum Disorder and Developmental Language Disorder is extremely limited in scope. For clarification purposes, Developmental Language Disorder was formerly named Specific Language Impairment. Comprehension underpins daily social interactions as individuals must be able to formulate inferences about other people's emotional reactions and provide appropriate responses (Ford and Milosky, 2003). Loukusa *et al.* (2014) studied social perception abilities in children with ASD, children with SLI, and typically de-veloping children. A battery of standardised language assessments was used as well as the Affect Recognition and Theory of Mind subtests from the Developmental Neuropsychological

Assessment – Second Edition (NEPSY-II, Korkman *et al.*, 2008). Children are assessed on their ability to correctly match basic emotions and neutral expressions in photographs of children's faces during the Affect Recognition task. Happy, sad, angry, afraid, and disgusted were the five basic emotions included in the subtest. Children with ASD performed significantly worse than children with SLI and typically developing children during the affect recognition tasks (Loukusa *et al.*, 2014). Notably, the children with SLI did not differ from the typically developing children when they were assessed on their emotion recognition abilities (Loukusa *et al.*, 2014). Together, these findings provide support to the view that emotion recognition deficits are associated with ASD.

The Theory of Mind subtest consisted of two components: a verbal task and a non-verbal, contextual task. Firstly, the verbal task consisted of children being presented with verbal scenarios, with and without supporting images. Children were then assessed on their responses to a series of questions about the scenarios, designed to measure their understanding of beliefs, intentions, other people's thoughts, ideas, and their comprehension of figurative language (Loukusa *et al.*, 2014). Interestingly, children with ASD and children with SLI did not differ from one-another during the verbal task measuring theory of mind (Loukusa *et al.*, 2014). Both groups, however, performed significantly worse than the typically developing children. One reasonable suggestion put forward by Loukusa *et al.* (2014) is that the ability to formulate inferences is often required during verbal tasks measuring theory of mind, and this has been found to be poor in SLI. Secondly, the contextual task consisted of presenting children with a selection of drawings depicting children in social contexts. Each image contained a character whose face was deliberately not shown. Four images were then presented to the children, with each one containing different emotions depicted on the chosen characters face. Children were then asked to select a corresponding emotion, hereby testing their ability to accurately infer the characters emotion based on social context alone (Loukusa *et al.*, 2014). No group differences emerged during the contextual task. This finding, however, may have been as a result of the contextual task being too simplistic unlike multifaceted social contexts in real-life situations (Loukusa *et al.*, 2014). For children with SLI, a correlation was reported between the verbal task, measuring theory of mind, and the Grammatical Closure subtest of Illinois Test of Psycholinguistic Abilities (ITPA, Kirk *et al.*, 1968) and the Test of Word Finding – Second Edition (TWF-2, German, 2000) (Loukusa *et al.*, 2014, p. 503). No correlation was detected between performance during the affect recognition task and language tests for children with SLI. For children with ASD, a moderate correlation was detected between performance during the theory of mind verbal task and the Test of Word Finding – Second Edition (German, 2000), although it narrowly missed reaching statistical significance (Loukusa *et al.*, 2014, p. 503). No correlations were detected for the typically developing children. Although Loukusa *et al.*'s (2014, p. 501) study yields interesting findings, the results should be interpreted with caution as the findings were based on small sample sizes; there were 18 children with SLI, 14 children with ASD, and 25 typically developing children.

Taylor *et al.* (2015) investigated emotion recognition abilities in children with Autism Spectrum Disorder and normal language skills (ALN), Autism Spectrum Disorder and a language impairment (ALI), and Specific Language Impairment (SLI). Surprise and disgust are classed as basic emotions under Ekman's (1992) theory; however, these were classed as complex emotions in Taylor *et al.*'s (2015) study on the basis that they involve inferring another person's mental state. Happy, sad, angry, and scared were categorised as simple emotions in the study. Children were presented with photographs of people with one of the six emotions depicted on their face during the visual task. During the auditory task, children listened to recordings of the sentence *Oh, I'm going out of the room now, but I'll be back later.* Variations of this were uttered to convey one of the six emotions. After each emotional expression, children were presented with a series of cartoon faces during the visual and auditory tasks. They then had to choose which emotion was expressed through selecting a cartoon image with a corresponding facial expression. Although children with Autism Spectrum Disorder and normal language skills (ALN) were able to correctly identify simple emotions during both the visual and auditory tasks, their difficulties lay with being able to identify complex emotional expressions. Interestingly, children with Autism Spectrum Disorder and a language impairment (ALI) and children with Specific Language Impairment (SLI) had difficulties in identifying simple and complex emotions during the visual and auditory emotion recognition tasks. This finding indicates that emotion recognition abilities may be influenced by language proficiency. Considering that children with ALI and children with SLI have language difficulties, it is plausible to suggest that they may not have acquired the linguistic proficiency which is essential to understand emotional information (Taylor *et al.*, 2015). For example, children with ALI and children with SLI may not have acquired the vocabulary for mental state verbs. Interestingly, the children with ALI and children with SLI's performance during the auditory emotion recognition task was poor; this led Taylor *et al.* (2015) to propose that both groups may have a shared deficit in understanding affective prosody. The significance of distinguishing between ALN and ALI is reinforced as through doing so, Taylor *et al.* (2015) was able to elicit discrepancies in emotion recognition abilities between the two groups. The results from this study reveal that the ALN, ALI, and SLI groups all exhibited emotion recognition difficulties.

Chapter 4.   Speech and Language

Speech incorporates language and the terms are often used interchangeably. They can, however, be distinguished from one-another. Speech is defined as the vocal production of sounds used as a method of communicating therefore it concerns features such as prosody, articulation, voice, and fluency. Language, however, can occur in either the spoken, written or signed form. Thus, speech impairments can be distinguished from language impairments although it is needless to say that they can co-occur.

4.1   The Five Components of Language

There are five basic components of language: syntax, phonology, morphology, semantics, and pragmatics. Throughout the world, there are many different languages used by a cohort of people who have a shared understanding of underlying representations. Each language has its own set of rules and principles underpinning it, and syntax is the study of how these words, phrases, and clauses are arranged to create sentences. Syntax is a component of grammar; this is finite as the human brain has a limited capacity of information which it is able to process and store (Chomsky and Halle, 1968). There are no restrictions on the number of sentences that can be constructed in any human language, nor are there restrictions on how meanings can be expressed as language is constantly evolving (Chomsky and Halle, 1968; Cruse, 2004). Phonology is another component of language, concerned with the study of the systematic organisation of speech sounds (Davenport and Hannahs, 2013). Morphemes are defined as the smallest unit of meaning in a language (Saxton, 2012). Free morphemes are single words which can stand alone, such as *tree* or *flower*, whereas bound morphemes, cannot stand alone therefore they must be attached to a lexical stem (Saxton, 2012). The meaning of language concerns semantics, which focuses on the literal interpretation of a sentence. There are two dominant approaches governing the field of semantics: the objectivist and mentalist view. According to the objectivist view, the meaning of a linguistic expression can be understood through values such as truths and falsities (Williams, 2015). Thus, semantics does not concern the mind according to the objectivist view. Contrary to this, the mentalist view proposes that all values are concepts or thoughts which originate in the mind (Williams, 2015). Pragmatics is also an important component which must be considered as it is concerned with the study of language use in contextual circumstances. It is important to note that pragmatics extends beyond the literal interpretation of language, taking a speaker's intentions into consideration even though this may not be explicitly vocalised. Language comprehension can be attributed to linguistic competence as an individual must have learned the syntactic, phonological, morphological, and semantic rules governing language. Communicative competence is also a fundamental part of language comprehension as it connects language use and contextual situations (Gleason, 2005; Norbury, 2011). The role that pragmatics plays in aiding language comprehension should not be undermined as it allows for the formation of implications and inferences about the meaning of a person's utterance as it takes contextual factors into consideration (Lyons, 1981; Happé, 1994; Baron-Cohen, 1995; St. Clair *et al.*, 2011). Pragmatic abilities enable a person to understand humour as well as form a perspective from another person's point of view, which is fundamental during social interactions. 'Pragmatic development and skills are difficult to quantify and to portray in developmental terms in contrast with phonological, lexical or grammatical abilities' (Tomblin, 2011, p. 129).

4.2   Chomsky's Theory of Universal Grammar

Chomsky is a pioneering linguist who is renowned for his work. The theory of universal grammar is one of Chomsky's (2002) most notable works; this postulates that all human beings possess an internal cognitive mechanism situated in the brain, known as the language faculty, which allows for the innate ability to acquire language. This ties in with language being a neurobiological function and, according to the theory of universal grammar, there is a system of universal rules governing language. These rules consist of syntactic, phonological, and semantic representations (Chomsky and Halle, 1968). The aforementioned representations are applicable to any human language and they work in conjunction with one-another. For example, the syntactic component contains an underlying deep structure and a surface structure; phonological representations are consigned to the surface structure whereas semantic representations form the deep structure (Chomsky and Halle, 1968). The underlying semantic representations are influenced by the phonological representation to some extent as a listener must first decode the speaker's auditory output to form an interpretation about the meaning of an utterance (Chomsky and Halle, 1986; Chomsky, 2006).

A speaker and a listener mentally construct phonological representations which determines their performance in being able to comprehend and produce language (Chomsky and Halle, 1968, p. 14). An utterance is defined as a unit of speech; this may consist of a single word, phrase, sentence, or a number of sentences combined. Utterances can be distinguished from sentences, with the latter defined as a combination of words formulated to create a grammatically complete expression (Oxford English Dictionary, 1989). Phonological features, such as intonation, are embedded within a speaker's production of an utterance and it can influence a listener's interpretation of a speaker's underlying intentions which may not be explicitly expressed. Thus, phonology and pragmatics work in conjunction with one another to derive meaning. Intonation concerns the rise and falls of a speaker's voice during the production of speech and it plays an important role during communication as variations in a speaker's intonation can be used to convey feelings or attitudes. For example, a speaker may express their surprise through uttering the interjection *oh* with rising and falling intonation. Also, a speaker may convey their negative emotional state, such as disappointment, through uttering *oh* with a falling intonation. Pitch is governed by the frequency of vibrations producing a sound and it refers to the perception of how high or low a sound is (Oxford English Dictionary, 2021). Pitch is a perceptual feature as a person forms an interpretation about the number of times the vocal cords vibrate per second, known as fundamental frequency (Davenport and Hannahs, 2013, p. 84). Pitch contour is a term which refers to a pattern of continuous variation in pitch; falling pitch contours can indicate a negative attitude whereas rising pitch contours can be used to express positivity (Davenport and Hannahs, 2013).

4.3   The Developmental Stages in the Acquisition of Language

The acquisition of language begins in the womb during embryogenesis as embryos are exposed to their own mother's voice and sounds in their environment (Sutton, 2017). During this time, babies are exposed to different tones produced during speech (National Health Service, no date). From birth, babies can express a positive and negative emotion: contentment and distress (Sutton, 2017). Within the first six months, infants develop the ability to control muscles required for talking which enables them to produce cooing sounds such as *ooh* and *aah* (National Health Service, no date.). It is worth highlighting that *ooh* and *aah* are both interjections, defined as an utterance expressing emotion. *Ooh* and *aah* are among the first words uttered by infants, highlighting their significance as holophrastic utterances and their notable feature within the early stages of language development. With this in mind, it can be argued that interjections are an integral part of language as children acquire interjections before they are able to produce fully-fledged sentences. Around the age of six months, infants begin to babble, and they start to repeat consonant and vowel syllables such as *mama* and *dada* (Rapin, 1996, p. 644). Single words are typically produced during the first year of life. Thus, children obtain an understanding of how to divide streams of sound into segments which carry meaning, demonstrating the connection between phonological representations and semantics. This process requires formulating associations between sounds and stimuli in the surrounding environment in order to formulate the meaning of a word (Rapin, 1996).

During the second year of life children acquire individual words and they begin to produce two-word or longer utterances once their lexicon has increased (Rapin, 1996). During the third year, the size of an infant's lexicon expands significantly as they acquire hundreds of words. The production of two-word utterances into sentences typically occurs during the third year of a child's life, paving the way for the evolution of syntactic knowledge (Rapin, 1996). The process of acquiring language involves both comprehension and production, although comprehension precedes production. With an expanding lexicon, children can then begin to understand and produce more complex sentences from the age of three years (Rapin, 1996). Children begin to acquire words which express their feelings and other mental states including wants, thoughts, needs, and desires from the age of two years old (Cross, 2011, p. 19). An example of this would be *I want a biscuit*. The verb *want* is classed as a cognitive term as it is used by a speaker to express their desire for something they are not in possession of. Although children initially express their own mental states and thoughts, they begin to attribute these to other people by the time they reach the age of three years (Cross, 2011, p. 19). The ability to recognise one's own mental states, as well as being able to attribute mental states to other people, is known as theory of mind and typically developing children acquire these abilities during the early stages of development. Theory of mind is a fundamental part of communication as it can be used to formulate inferences and make predictions about another person's behaviour, as well as allowing for the interpretation of other people's actions (Premack and Woodruff, 1978; Happé, 1994; Tager-Flusberg and Sullivan, 1995). Thus, theory of mind is 'a mechanism which underlies a crucial aspect of social skills' (Baron-Cohen *et al.*, 1985, p. 38). Children have also been found to recognise another person's mental state through providing comfort to other people in distress at the age of 3 years, as well as beginning to partake in deception which obscures the truth (Wellman, 2014, p. 3). Children tend to have acquired the rules which govern their native language by the age of four, as well as having developed written language skills (Rapin, 1996, p. 645). The former involves mastering the syntactic, phonological, morphological, and semantic rules which underpin a language (Gleason, 2005). Thus, a diagnosis of language disorder should only be considered from the age of four years old as language tends to have stabilised in typically developing children around this age (Bishop and

Edmundson, 1987). The developmental stages outlined may be applicable to the acquisition of interjections; for example, it is plausible to suggest that children produce interjections expressing their own internal mental states before developing the skills to attribute states to others.

4.4   Language as a tool for Communicating and Interacting

Language primarily serves a communicative purpose. According to Sperber and Wilson (1995), there are two forms of communication: the code model and the inferential model. The code model consists of encoding and decoding messages, whereas the inferential model refers to producing and interpreting messages as demonstrated in Figure 4. A person must first be able to decode a message in order to form an interpretation about its meaning (Sperber and Wilson, 1995). The code model is not sufficient in being able to explain human communication alone therefore it must interact with the inferential model to allow for successful communication (Baron-Cohen, 1995).

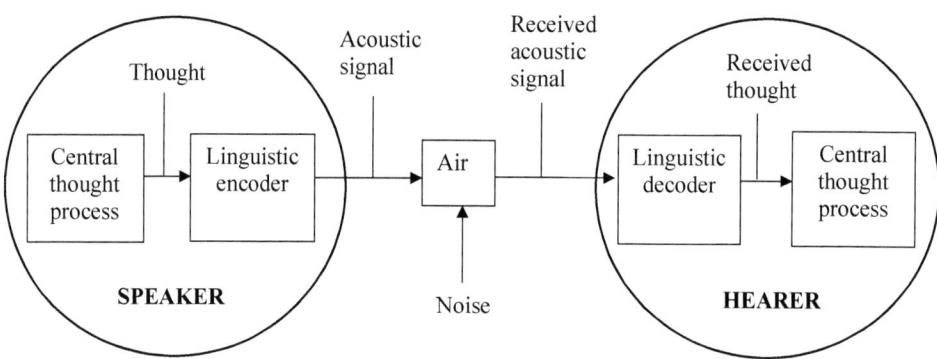

Figure 4. A representation of the code model of human communication (Sperber and Wilson, 1995, p. 5)

Communication is defined as the exchange of information, knowledge, and ideas which are intended to convey a message (Oxford English Dictionary, 2009). Thus, communication can be used to fulfil a range of different functions such as expressing meanings, thoughts, propositions, beliefs, attitudes, and emotions (Sperber and Wilson, 1995). These are all abstract mental states which are represented by an internal cognitive mechanism underlying behaviour

28

(Happé, 1994; Baron-Cohen, 1995). There are two methods of communication: non-verbal and verbal. There are many different types of non-verbal methods of communication: some examples include facial expressions, gestures, eye contact, and body language. According to Sperber and Wilson (1995), non-verbal communication is implicit as it cannot be expressed through vocalisations. On the other hand, verbal expressions are explicit as the production of speech sounds, vocalisations, and language can all be used to express meaning (Sperber and Wilson, 1995). Consequently, it can be argued that vocalisations are the most efficient form of communication (Darwin, 1872; Sperber and Wilson, 1995). This can be supported by the fact that individuals are exposed to auditory sounds in their surrounding environment whereas non-verbal methods of communication can be averted. For example, a person may focus their eye gaze elsewhere to minimise or avoid making eye contact with another person.

Communication forms part of the triad of impairments in ASD. With regard to non-verbal methods of communication, previous studies have reported that individuals with ASD have difficulty decoding facial expressions during emotion recognition tasks (Loukusa *et al.*, 2014; Taylor *et al.*, 2015). Additionally, some individuals with ASD may avoid sustaining eye contact (American Psychiatric Association, 2013). However, this is not a universal characteristic of ASD. Some individuals with ASD are able to sustain eye contact, although they may exhibit other non-verbal deficits used for the purposes of social communication (American Psychiatric Association, 2013, p. 54). Vocalisations can be accompanied by non-verbal gestures therefore they can be entwined, such as nodding your head while uttering *yes* to indicate agreement. Some individuals with ASD may have difficulties in being able to understand and interpret language as it is primarily used for a communicative purpose (Parikh, 2000). Deficits in language comprehension can impact upon a person's communicative abilities and engagement in social interactions as they may find it difficult to understand and interpret linguistic expressions used in everyday situations. Consequently, they may struggle with initiating, responding to, and sustaining conversations with other people (Kjellmer *et al.*, 2012).

Difficulties in being able to attribute mental states to oneself and to other people may impede upon a person partaking in social interactions (Andrés-Roqueta *et al.*, 2013). Human beings have a tendency to discuss their emotional and mental states with other people during social interactions which can lead to the development and sustainability of some relationships. Fewer social interactions can impact upon the development of social and cognitive abilities (Andrés-Roqueta *et al.*, 2013). Considering that ASD and Language Disorder are both classed as communication disorders in the DSM-5 (American Psychiatric Association, 2013), difficulties can lead to a person becoming increasingly frustrated, particularly if they do not have the linguistic abilities required to express the message which they are trying to convey. Thus, it can make it difficult for a listener to form an interpretation about the meaning of a speaker's utterance. Delayed language comprehension is a feature associated with ASD, and it is apparent in individuals even without an intellectual disability (Rapin, 1996; Kjellmer *et al.*, 2012; Kover *et al.*, 2014). Similarly, Language Disorder is diagnosed according to a person presenting with comprehension and/or production deficits in the absence of an intellectual impairment.

Some individuals with ASD can have an accompanying language impairment, however it is not a universal deficit as the linguistic abilities of those with ASD is extensive (Kjelgaard and Tager-Flusberg, 2001). For example, some individuals with ASD may be non-verbal or their speech may be extremely limited whereas others demonstrate proficient language skills (Kjelgaard and Tager-Flusberg, 2001; American Psychiatric Association, 2013). Although vocabulary and grammar may be intact for some individuals with ASD, their use of language for social communicative purposes may be impaired (American Psychiatric Association, 2013). Some individuals with ASD are able to talk in length about a certain topic they are interested in, however difficulties lay in turn-taking and holding a conversation between two or more people. Interests that are highly restricted, fixated and abnormal in intensity is a behavioural characteristic of ASD (American Psychiatric Association, 2013, p. 50). For instance, an individual with ASD may show immense interest in modes of transport and they may possess the linguistic abilities to be able to talk in great detail about transport timetables, routes, and services. Idiosyncratic language is also a feature of language associated with ASD and it is defined as 'the use of conventional words or phrases in unusual ways to convey specific meanings' (Volden and Lord, 1991, p. 111). Idiosyncratic language can make it difficult for a listener to decode the message that a speaker is trying to communicate, particularly when a word or phrase is over-extended in its use and/or an alternative meaning is applied. A primary example of this can be exemplified through an observation I made of a child with ASD repeatedly uttering the word *sad* while continuously pressing down upon a sink tap, allowing water to flow from it. The principal semantic meaning of the word *sad* refers to the emotional state of feeling sorrowful or regret (Oxford English Dictionary, 2008). Water taps are inanimate objects therefore they cannot experience emotional states. Thus, a listener must be able to decode and form an interpretation about the intended meaning of a speaker's utterance by consenting the inferential process using the information available (Surian *et al.*, 1996). A person must take into consideration any existing contextual circumstances when formulating an interpretation about the meaning of a speaker's utterance as language can be ambiguous. Thus, a person must apply their own knowledge of the world to be able to interpret language use in relation to context. This led Sperber and Wilson (1986) to propose that pragmatic inferences are more influential than consulting the literal semantic interpretations of language to allow for successful communication.

Although structural language abilities are variable in ASD, pragmatics is a universal deficit (Taylor *et al.*, 2015). Pragmatics is a fundamental part of communication as it allows a person to form inferences about speaker's utterances. Pragmatics is essential in order to 'disambiguate lexical terms, interpret deictic terms, integrate contextual information, and recover propositional attitudes, thereby compute implicit meaning' (Surian *et al.*, 1996, p. 57). Referring back to the observation I made of a child with ASD uttering the word *sad* as water simultaneously poured out of the tap, the context must be taken into consideration in order to decipher meaning. As sad is an emotional state conveying negative valence, it can be plausibly suggested that the meaning of the word *sad* was over-extended to formulate a connection between crying whereby tears are produced, the emotional state of feeling sad, and water. The expressive language abilities of the child with ASD in reference were limited therefore the over-extension of *sad* may have been used to communicate water was pouring out of the tap. Additionally, the child with ASD also had a tendency to frequently utter the phrase *baby dragon sad* in the absence of a stimulus. This is a good illustration of idiosyncratic language which is characteristic of autism. Although typically developing children over-extend words as their language undergoes development, this usually resolves around the age of three years as lexicon expands (Cross, 2011).

4.5   The Relationship between Language and Theory of Mind

The interrelation between language and theory of mind can be demonstrated through neurology. Theory of mind is a component of neural anatomy which allows for a person to form an understanding about social interactions, communication, and behaviour (Baron-Cohen, 1995). Also known as mind-blindness, theory of mind is associated with several regions of the brain including the temporoparietal junction, the posterior medial cortex, and the medial prefrontal cortex (Clark *et al.*, 2018). The temporoparietal junction is a region of the brain where the temporal and parietal lobes meet. As previously stated in chapter two, Wernicke's area is located in the posterior region of the superior temporal gyrus and it controls the perception of speech (Clark *et al.*, 2018). Broca's area, composed of pars opercularis and pars triangularis, is located in the prefrontal cortex and it controls the production of language.

Theory of mind and language abilities are interlinked as a person must be able to process and understand a speaker's utterance as well as recognise and attribute mental states to other people, allowing for successful communication. It is now well established from a variety of studies that pragmatics is a universal impairment in ASD (American Psychiatric Association, 2000; Bishop, 1989; Surian *et al.*, 1996; Andrés-Roqueta and Katsos, 2017; Tesink *et al.*, 2009; Weismer, 2013). Theory of mind deficits have been postulated to account for the pragmatic difficulties which are characteristic of ASD including difficulties in comprehending linguistic expressions conveying non-literal meanings such as irony, sarcasm, humour, and metaphors (Baron-Cohen, 1995). The literal semantic meaning of an utterance cannot always be taken at face value, especially when some speakers do not always mean what they say.

4.5.1 False-belief tasks as a measurement of Theory of Mind

There is a tendency for children with ASD to perform worse than typically developing children during tasks measuring theory of mind abilities (Baron-Cohen *et al.*, 1985; Happé, 1995; Losh and Capps, 2003; Tager-Flusberg, 2011). One of the most well-known tools for assessing theory of mind abilities consists of using false-belief tasks. The two most common types are the Sally-Anne and Smarties tasks. To clarify, the Sally-Anne false-belief task involves using two dolls, named Sally and Anne, who are presented to a child. One of the dolls, Sally, has a basket whereas the other doll, Anne, is in possession of a box. The first step in this process involves Sally putting a marble into her basket and then she proceeds to leave the room. While Sally is absent, Anne transfers the marble from Sally's basket and puts it into her box. This is depicted in Figure 5. When Sally returns, the child is asked three questions measuring belief, reality, and memory. Firstly, the belief question involves asking the child where Sally will look for her marble. The child must state that Sally will look for the marble in her basket in order to pass the belief question thereby demonstrating they have acknowledged Sally's false belief. Secondly, the reality question involves asking the child where the marble is located. Finally, the memory question involves asking the child where the marble was located at the beginning of the task (Baron-Cohen *et al.*, 1985).

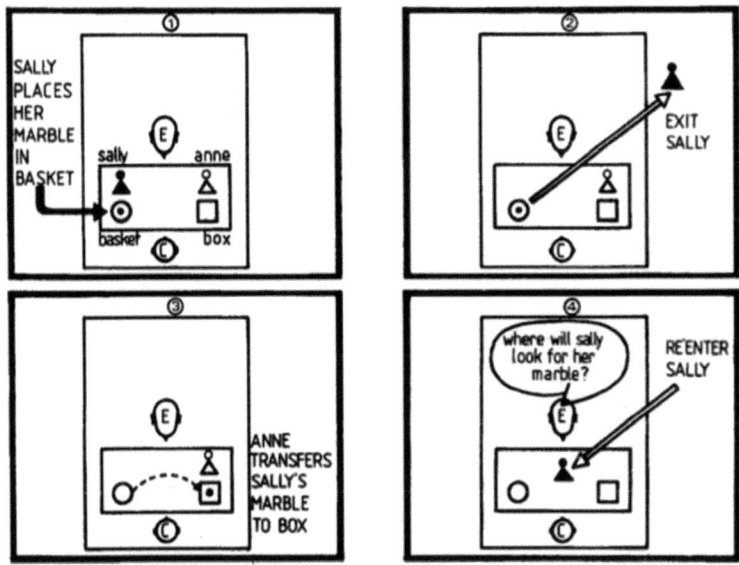

Figure 5. A representation of the Sally-Anne false-belief task (Baron-Cohen _et al._, 1985, p. 41)

Previous research has established that some children with ASD are able to pass false-belief tasks (Happé, 1995; Tager-Flusberg and Sullivan, 1995; Losh and Capps, 2003). A study conducted by Baron-Cohen _et al._ (1985, p. 42) reported that 16 out of 20 individuals with autism failed the false belief task during two trials; this consisted of the Sally-Anne task and the introduction of a new object location being the experimenter's pocket. Thus, four individuals with autism passed the false-belief tasks albeit it is a small minority. One possible explanation for this is that the verbal mental ages for the four children and adolescents with autism who passed both false-belief tasks was higher than the remaining 16 participants with autism who were not successful. Closer examination reveals that the verbal mental ages of the four children and adolescents with autism who passed both tasks ranged from 2.9 years to 7 years, notably lower than their chronological ages which were between 10.11 to 15.10 years (Baron-Cohen _et al._, 1985, p. 42). Baron-Cohen _et al._'s (1985) study has been largely influential as it paved the way for many researchers to replicate false-belief tasks to measure theory of mind abilities within clinical populations. There are, however, some limitations which must be addressed. Firstly, the age range for the children and adolescents with autism and Down's syndrome, who formed two distinct groups, was more extensive compared to the typically developing children. For example, the age range of the groups in Baron-Cohen _et al._'s (1985, p. 40) study were as follows: autism (6.1 years to 16.6 years), Down's syndrome (6.3 years to 17 years old), and typically developing children (3.5 years to 5.9 years old). Thus, the participants were not matched accordingly. The non-verbal and verbal mental ages were not calculated for the typically developing children therefore it was not possible to investigate comparisons between the three groups based on this. Furthermore, the biological sex of the participants was not specified in Baron-Cohen et al.'s (1985) study; as a result, it cannot be deciphered whether there was a significant discrepancy between the number of male and female participants. Considering that language plays a fundamental part in theory of mind development, it can be hypothesised that children with ASD who have proficient language abilities have a higher chance of passing false-belief tasks. A study conducted by Happé (1995) supports this claim as individuals with autism required significantly higher verbal abilities to pass theory of mind tasks compared to typically developing individuals and mentally handicapped individuals. The Sally-Anne and Smarties false-belief tasks were used in the aforementioned study and the British Picture Vocabulary Scale was used to measure verbal mental ages. The results of Happé's (1995, p. 850) study revealed that individuals with autism whose verbal mental ages were below 5.6 years were unable to pass both false-belief tasks. It is worth noting that four individuals with autism passed both false-belief tasks, although their verbal mental ages were above 11.7 years (Happé, 1995, p. 850). By contrast, the typically developing cohort required a verbal mental age of 2.10 years to be able to pass theory of mind tasks (Happé, 1995, p. 851). These findings can be used to support an intrinsic link between language and theory of mind abilities.

One criticism of much of the literature on false-belief tasks is that there is a tendency for researchers to recruit participants with ASD whose language abilities are classed as being within the normal range. As previously stated, at least half of all children with ASD have intellectual disabilities (Mody and Belliveau, 2013, p. 158). Thus, a large proportion of the autistic population are omitted from research. This is noteworthy considering that an ac-companying language impairment is commonplace in ASD. Further research should be carried out to establish whether there are any discrepancies between language abilities and theory of mind development in ASD and ASD-LI as this provides scope for a more insightful overview of language abilities across the autistic spectrum. To date, much of the available literature investigating theory of mind abilities has focused on Autism Spectrum Disorder. By contrast, the number of studies researching theory of mind abilities using children with a language impairment is extremely limited in scope (Farrar et al., 2009; Andrés-Roqueta et al., 2013;

Spanoudis, 2016). Further work should be undertaken to investigate the relationship between language and theory of mind abilities with individuals diagnosed with a language impairment. This is an important issue for future research. For example, Andrés-Roqueta *et al.* (2013) showed that children with Specific Language Impairment (SLI) do not perform as well as typically developing children during false belief tasks, even though both groups were matched according to chronological age and language abilities. Thus, these factors cannot account for differences in group performance. For the children with SLI, the average age in which they were able to pass false-belief tasks was 5.4 years (Andrés-Roqueta *et al.*, 2013, p. 734). This finding is noteworthy considering that the children with autism in Happé's (1995) study required a verbal mental age of 5.6 years before they were able to pass false-belief tasks. The findings from these studies can be used in conjunction with one-another to reinforce the suggestion that children with communication disorders require a higher verbal mental age to pass theory of mind tasks compared to their typically developing peers. Further research should be undertaken to investigate theory of mind abilities using individuals with Autism Spectrum Disorder and individuals with a language disorder to discern whether theory of mind is a universal impairment in ASD or whether it is a deficit associated with neurodevelopmental disorders affecting communication, such as DLD. The severity of language impairment may also influence performance on theory of mind tasks as children with a moderate language impairment performed significantly worse than those with a mild impairment in Farrar *et al.*'s (2009) study.

Chapter 5. Narratives

Narratives are defined as an account of a sequence of events which occur in a logical order, and they often contain references to characters internal states (Stein and Glen, 1975). A narrative is a story, and it plays a fundamental role in social interactions and human communication (Duinmeijer *et al.*, 2012; Norbury *et al.*, 2014; Siller *et al.*, 2014). Telling and retelling stories are a part of everyday life as human beings share their experiences with others and make sense of the world around them. From an early age, children are encouraged to read books and tell stories. Narratives are an integral part of the education system and they are an effective tool as they can be used to teach children about a range of different topics. Storytelling can also be used by children and adults as a method for establishing, developing, and sustaining relationships with other people (Wetherell *et al.*, 2007; Siller *et al.*, 2014). Considering that narratives have an interactional purpose when they are used in discourse contexts, difficulties in being able to formulate a story can have an impact upon a person's social-emotional and communicative abilities (Losh and Capps, 2003; Duinmeijer *et al.*, 2012; Norbury *et al.*, 2014). Social-emotional skills refers to a person's ability to express and manage their internal mental states including their thoughts, feelings, and emotions as well as being able to attribute mental states to other people.

Narratives can occur in the form of spoken or written accounts, as well as being depicted through a series of visual illustrations. There are two elements which narratives are usually composed of: the setting, and an episode or event (Stein and Glen, 1975). The setting typically occurs at the beginning of a story and the main characters are often introduced within this frame, although additional characters may be introduced throughout (Stein and Glen, 1975). The setting can also include references to the social, physical, or temporal context which helps to set the scene for the remaining part of the story to follow (Stein and Glen, 1975). References to characters internal states are often incorporated within an episode; this may include characters cognitive states, emotions, and their intentions, all of which can influence their behaviour (Stein and Glen, 1975). The term cognition refers to the action or faculty of knowing therefore it incorporates thoughts, sensations, and perceptions (Oxford English Dictionary, 1989). *Decide*, *know*, and *wonder* are all examples of cognitive terms.

Narratives can provide an insight into a person's cognitive, social, and linguistic abilities (Tager-Flusberg and Sullivan, 1995; Capps et al., 2000; Losh and Capps, 2003; Norbury and Bishop, 2003; Reilly et al., 2004; Norbury et al., 2014). Internal mental states are composed of a person's knowledge, beliefs, feelings, intentions, and desires; the ability to attribute these to other people can help to predict and explain the behaviour and actions of other people (Norbury and Bishop, 2003). This is known as theory of mind, as previously addressed in chapter four. Thus, storytelling is an insightful way of measuring a child's ability to understand other people and the world around them. Within a narrative, the internal states of characters may not be explicit therefore the narrator must be able to connect elements of the story together cohesively and draw inferences to create a story which has meaning (Norbury and Bishop, 2003). Thus, a narrator must be able to use their spatial and temporal knowledge to establish and recognise causes between events (Norbury and Bishop, 2003; Duinmeijer et al., 2012; Norbury et al., 2014). The process of constructing a story involves linguistic skills as a narrator must understand the syntactic, phonological, morphological, semantic, and pragmatic components of language to be able to construct sentences and utterances which carry meaning. Children must have grasped all the aforementioned linguistic skills to become proficient at storytelling.

Narrative tasks are fruitful in providing an insight into a person's linguistic abilities, although it is worth noting that generating a story measures a person's expressive abilities rather than their comprehension of language (Tager Flusberg and Sullivan, 1995). To date, the number of studies investigating narrative comprehension is extremely limited in scope. Fuijiki et al. (2008) reported that children with a language impairment were not as proficient as their typically developing peers when they were tested on their comprehension of prosodic cues conveying a range of different emotions while listening to a personal narrative. There were only four emotions investigated and the outcome consisted of happiness being the most accurately identified by both groups followed by anger, sadness, and fear (Fujiki et al., 2008, p. 339). This is in line with previous studies which have reported that happiness is the most easily identifiable emotion (Ford and Milosky, 2003; Castelli, 2005). Narrative comprehension was also investigated by Blom and Boerma (2016) who found that children with SLI performed worse than their typically developing peers when they were asked a series of questions after listening to a story.

There have been several techniques adopted in previous studies measuring narrative abilities including the following: retelling a story (Manolitsi and Botting, 2011), generating a story through conversational prompts which is reminiscent of unstructured daily interactions (Capps *et al.*, 2000; Losh and Capps, 2003; Wetherell *et al.*, 2007), generating a story using a series of pictures, acting as a visual prompt (Colozzo *et al.*, 2011), and wordless picture books (Tager-Flusberg and Sullivan, 1995; Capps *et al.*, 2000; Losh and Capps, 2003; Norbury and Bishop, 2003; Reilly *et al.*, 2004; Wetherell *et al.*, 2007; Norbury *et al.*, 2014; Siller *et al.*, 2014; Banney *et al.*, 2015). Narrative generation tasks also feature in some clinical assessments, such as The Autism Diagnostic Observation Schedule (ADOS). Further, The Renfrew Bus Story Test is a standardised assessment used to measure narrative abilities, although it is only suitable for use with children aged between 5 and 8 years old. One of the most well-known tools for assessing narrative abilities is the use of wordless picture books as it requires a narrator to infer characters facial expressions, their gestures, the setting, event, and actions from visual illustrations depicted. The benefit of this approach is that it provides an insight into a person's understanding of a story (Serafini, 2014). Also, a major advantage of using wordless picture books is that they provide an opportunity for the elicitation of language.

5.1 Arguments for Narratives to be used as a Clinical Tool

Story generation is one task used in the Autism Diagnostic Observation Schedule – Generic (ADOS-G); this is a standardised assessment used to measure social interaction, communication, play, and imaginative use of materials which is administered to individuals suspected of meeting criteria for a diagnosis of autism or other pervasive developmental disorders (Lord *et al.*, 2000). The ADOS-G is composed of four modules based on expressive language abilities and the examiner must select the most appropriate module to administer. Wordless picture books are used for the story generation task in the ADOS-G, although storytelling is restricted to two modules as it is linguistically demanding (Lord *et al.*, 2000). Thus, the story generation task appears in Module 3 which is administered to children who have fluent speech and Module 4, suitable for adolescents and adults who are also verbally fluent (Lord *et al.*, 2000). Although story generation is one element of the ADOS-G, the narratives produced are not usually analysed for their content or structure (Banney *et al.*, 2015).

Narratives can provide an insight into a child's progress and development over time, whereas raw scores on standardised tests may not be able to encapsulate this (Manolitsi and Botting, 2011). There is a growing body of literature that recognises the importance of introducing narratives for use as a clinical tool on the premise that they are sensitive enough to be able to detect linguistic difficulties which standardised language assessments may not pick up on (Capps *et al.*, 2000; Wetherell *et al.*, 2007; Manolitsi and Botting, 2011; Banney *et al.*, 2015). This is demonstrated in a study conducted by Siller *et al.* (2014) as they reported that children with ASD produced fewer utterances, words, and references to internal states and characters emotions compared to typically developing children when telling a story. The children with ASD also used a more limited range of different verbs and adjectives compared to the typically developing cohort (Siller *et al.*, 2014). These notable differences were reported despite matching the children with ASD and the typically developing children based upon their receptive and expressive language abilities, as well as intelligent quotient scores. The Peabody Picture Vocabulary Test – Fourth Edition (Dunn and Dunn, 2007) was used to measure receptive vocabulary, whereas the Expressive One Word Picture Vocabulary Test – Fourth Edition (Brownell, 2000) was used to measure expressive language abilities. The findings from Siller *et al.*'s (2014) study indicate that linguistic and cognitive abilities cannot account for the discrepancies in narrative performance between the two groups.

With regard to language, narratives provide an insight into a person's pragmatic abilities as context plays an important role during their production (Capps *et al.*, 2000; Norbury and Bishop, 2003; Norbury *et al.*, 2014). The advantage of using wordless picture books to measure narrative and linguistic abilities is that they do not contain any written text, therefore the narrator has to form an inference about what is happening in the story based upon the illustrations depicted and the context. Narratives can be used as an intervention aimed to help improve and develop children's understanding of social situations and pragmatic skills (Capps *et al.*, 2000; Siller *et al.*, 2014). Social Stories™ are short narratives designed to help improve a child's understanding of certain situations, events, or activities (National Autistic Society, 2018). Narratives can also be used to support children's abilities to sequence events and form connections between them, as well as encourage children to formulate inferences about cha-racters internal states and make predictions about their behaviour. By doing so, there is the potential that narratives can have an impact upon a child's theory of mind abilities (Siller *et al.*, 2014). Considering that theory of mind is an impairment in ASD, it can be plausibly suggested that some individuals may find it difficult to interpret characters internal states as well as make predictions about their behaviour.

5.2   Factors affecting narrative performance

Narrative performance may be affected by several factors including attention, memory, and linguistic abilities. While a narrator is telling a story, they must ensure that their attention is maintained to ensure that they deliver the order of events coherently (Blom and Boerma, 2016). The perspectives of listeners must also be taken into consideration, as well as engaging with the audience to ensure that their attention is sustained (Reilly *et al.*, 2004). A listener can provide encouragement to the narrator by indicating that they are paying attention such as through nodding their head in agreement or producing phatic interjections such as *mm*, *okay*, and *yeah*. Phatic interjections play an important role during social interactions as they can be used to maintain social and communicative contact between a speaker and listener (Ameka, 1992). The topic of interjections will be explored in more depth in chapter six.

Narrative generation tasks have been used a considerable amount in previous studies, and there are many advantages of using this method to measure a person's linguistic abilities. Nevertheless, there are some limitations which must be considered. Firstly, if a person does not engage with a story, or if they demonstrate little or no interest in generating a story under task conditions, then there is the potential that their narrative performance will be distorted. For example, a person may produce shorter and fewer utterances to end the task imminently. By doing so, it may not provide a wholly accurate representation of a person's linguistic abilities. Secondly, another problem with using this method is that some children may be apprehensive about generating a story if they are mindful of their utterances being recorded.

The type of narrative task can influence a person's production of language to a certain degree. A study conducted by Capps *et al.* (2003) found that children with autism or Asperger syndrome (AS) and typically developing children told significantly longer stories when producing a personal narrative compared to telling a story using a wordless picture book. The personal narrative method involved engaging in a conversation with the researcher about their own interests. The children with autism or AS required significantly more prompts to elaborate upon their story compared to typically developing children during the personal narrative task, although this was not the case for the storybook task (Losh and Capps, 2003). A possible explanation is that the illustrations depicted in the wordless picture book could have acted as a supportive visual aid during the storytelling task, prompting the children with autism or AS to produce longer narratives. It should be noted that 20 out of the 28 children in the ASD group were identified as having Asperger Syndrome (Losh and Capps, 2003, p. 242). Although the DSM-5 (American Psychiatric Association, 2013) provides Autism Spectrum Disorder as a single classification, the International Classification of Diseases – 11th Revision (ICD-11, World Health Organization, 2019) subsumes Asperger Syndrome under the title of ASD without disorder of intellectual development and with mild or no impairment of functional language. In order to meet this criteria, a person's intellectual functioning and adaptive behaviour must be at least within the average range, approximately greater than the 2.3[rd] percentile (ICD-11, World Health Organization, 2019). All the children included in Losh and Capps' (2003, p. 242) study performed within the normal range of intelligence and were matched according to chronological age and verbal IQ, measured using the Wechsler Intelligence Scale for Children – Third Edition (WISC-III, 1991). As the children identified as having AS were not significantly impaired in their language abilities or cognitive development, it is plausible to suggest that they did not struggle to meet the demands of the task and they were therefore able to comprehend the instructions given. The children with AS also demonstrated proficient linguistic abilities; this may be used as a possible explanation for why no significant differences were reported in the length of narratives compared to the typically developing children.

Narratives can evoke emotions by the reader or listener. A primary example of this is an observation I made in the classroom context as the teacher read aloud the book *What a Bad Dog!* by Roderick Hunt and Alex Brychta to the class. The plotline consists of following a dog who embarks on a journey whilst simultaneously wreaking havoc, such as by running through concrete, mud, and pulling down a washing line with freshly laundered clothes on. The dog named Floppy is a character who originates from The Magic Key series, a popular collection of books among children. Floppy's owner becomes angry upon every mishap made, evident through Floppy being called a bad dog throughout the book. Upon listening to the teacher read aloud each of Floppy's mishaps, one child with ASD repeatedly produced the interjectional phrase *Oh no!* Taking the context into consideration, it can be proposed that *Oh no!* was used to express alarm at Floppy's actions. The significance of interjections can be demonstrated through their ability to convey the same communicative content as a longer utterance, as previously stated. In this case, the speaker produced *Oh no!* instead of explicitly stating *I am alarmed*. *Oh* is the most common interjection found in the English language, and it can often be found combined with words such as *dear, God, well, yes, no,* etc. to form secondary interjections (Stange, 2009, p. 57).

5.3 Narrative Production in Autism Spectrum Disorder

Narratives have been used in previous research with typically developing individuals, as well as with clinical populations including Autism Spectrum Disorder (Tager-Flusberg and Sullivan, 1995; Capps *et al.*, 2000; Losh and Capps, 2003; Norbury and Bishop, 2003; Manolitsi and Botting, 2011; Norbury *et al.*, 2014; Siller *et al.*, 2014; Banney *et al.*, 2015), individuals with mental retardation (Tager-Flusberg and Sullivan, 1995), developmental delays (Capps *et al.*, 2000), Williams Syndrome (Reilly *et al.*, 2004), Pragmatic Language Impairment (Botting, 2002; Norbury and Bishop, 2003), and Specific Language Impairment (Kaderavek and Sulzby, 2000; Botting, 2002; Norbury and Bishop, 2003; Reilly *et al.*, 2004; Wetherell *et al.*, 2007; Manolitsi and Botting, 2011; Duinmeijer *et al.*, 2012, Norbury *et al.*, 2014). As it was pointed out in the introduction of this book, some individuals with ASD can have an accompanying language impairment although it is not a universal characteristic of ASD. For example, some individuals with ASD demonstrate proficiency in being able to produce and comprehend language although difficulties using language to fulfil a social purpose may still arise as this forms part of the diagnostic criteria (Siller *et al.*, 2014; Volden *et al.*, 2017). Thus, the ability to formulate a narrative may be problematic even for individuals with high-functioning autism as storytelling is often used during social interactions therefore it has a discursive function (Siller *et al.*, 2014). Considering that pragmatics is a universal impairment in ASD, this element of narratives may pose a problem for such individuals with the disorder.

There have been inconsistent findings in regard to the production of narratives by children with ASD in comparison to a typically developing cohort. This discrepancy could be attributed to differences in the selection of participants, matching criteria, and methodological variations which can make it problematic when attempting to compare results. Prior studies have reported no significant differences in the length of narratives produced by children with ASD when compared to typically developing children (Losh and Capps, 2003). On the other hand, several studies have found that children with ASD produce shorter narratives compared to typically developing children (Capps *et al.*, 2000; Siller *et al.*, 2014), as well as use fewer utterances (Capps *et al.*, 2000; Siller *et al.*, 2014), use fewer words (Siller *et al.*, 2014), use limited complex syntax (Capps *et al.*, 2000; Banney *et al.*, 2015), and use a more limited range of verbs and adjectives (Siller *et al.*, 2014). Previous studies have also found that children with ASD use fewer references to characters internal states, including their emotions, compared to typically developing children when telling a story (Losh and Capps, 2003; Siller *et al.*, 2014).

Contrary to this, a number of studies have reported no significant differences between the use of internal state language by children with ASD and typically developing children (Norbury and Bishop, 2003; Norbury et al., 2014; Banney et al., 2015), including references to cognitive states (Tager-Flusberg and Sullivan, 1995; Capps et al., 2000; Norbury and Bishop, 2003; Siller et al., 2014; Banney et al., 2015), the number of emotion terms used (Tager-Flusberg and Sullivan, 1995; Norbury and Bishop, 2003; Banney et al., 2015) and evaluative devices during narrative production (Norbury and Bishop, 2003). Emotions are often visibly depicted on the facial expressions of characters therefore this may aid children's use of emotive terms during narrative tasks. Cognitive terms are not observable therefore a narrator must be able to form an interpretation about a character's mental state (Norbury and Bishop, 2003).

The ability to attribute mental states to other people is an integral feature of storytelling as it can be used to explain a character's behaviour and their actions as a result of their internal states (Tager-Flusberg and Sullivan, 1995; Capps et al., 2000; Norbury and Bishop, 2003; Norbury et al., 2014). Thus, story generation tasks are a particularly useful method in eliciting language which can be examined for references to frames of mind. Prior studies have found that children with ASD do not differ from typically developing children in the number of references to emotional and cognitive states produced when telling a story. For example, a study conducted by Tager-Flusberg and Sullivan (1995) reported that there were no significant differences between the number of emotive terms and references to behaviour used by individuals with ASD, individuals with mental retardation, and typically developing children when they produced a narrative using a wordless picture book. Mental retardation was the term used to refer to individuals with intellectual disabilities at the time of publication, however it has since been revised following legislative procedures. The participants were probed on the feeling states of six characters and asked to provide an explanation for their emotional states. Most participants, including the typically developing children, only used simple emotion terms during the task. One possible explanation for this is that the wordless picture book used may not have provided many opportunities for the elicitation of emotive terms. Nevertheless, individuals with autism performed significantly worse than the typically developing children when they were tested on their ability to provide an appropriate emotion in reference to the feeling states of characters in the story (Tager-Flusberg and Sullivan, 1995). This finding confirms that some individuals with autism are able to recognise and use simple emotive terms although the ability to provide an appropriate explanation for emotional states relative to context is a difficulty. This hereby reinforces that pragmatics is a universal impairment in ASD.

In their study, Tager-Flusberg and Sullivan (1995) reported no differences in the use of cognitive states produced by the individuals with ASD, individuals with mental retardation, and the typically developing children. A possible explanation is that the choice of book used during the storytelling task may not have provided many opportunities for the elicitation of cognitive states, hence why there were few references produced by all three groups. This is one disadvantage of using wordless picture books to measure narrative performance. To develop a full picture of a person's narrative abilities, future studies should incorporate a range of different narrative measures as this would allow for a more accurate representation. Referring back to Tager-Flusberg and Sullivan's (1995) study, the use of cognitive terms was significantly associated with performance on false-belief tasks for individuals with autism and individuals with mental retardation who were matched according to language abilities. This finding confirms the interrelation between theory of mind, language, and narrative abilities. However, there are some limitations which must be addressed. Firstly, the typically developing children in Tager-Flusberg and Sullivan's (1995) study were not subjected to participating in false-belief tasks, nor were language assessments and full-scale intelligent quotient scores obtained for this group. As a result, it is not possible to make comparisons between all three groups. Secondly, the method used for participation selection poses a problem as the typically developing children were recruited based upon their chronological age belonging in the same range as the mental ages of individuals with autism and individuals with mental retardation. Mental ages can vary considerably even in the typically developing population and no assessments were conducted by Tager-Flusberg and Sullivan (1995) to determine these. Thus, there is no guarantee that the chronological ages of the typically developing cohort corresponded to their mental age level. Although the individuals with autism and the individuals with mental retardation were matched according to language abilities, their mean chronological ages and full-scale intelligent quotient scores differed. Participants were not matched accordingly, which is another limitation of the study, as the mean chronological age of the typically developing children was significantly lower than the individuals with autism and individuals with mental retardation.

Similarly, Capps et al. (2000) found there were no significant group differences between the frequency of references made to character's affective and cognitive states by children with autism, developmental delays, and typically developing children when telling a story. This finding is in line with Tager-Flusberg and Sullivan's (1995) results. No group differences were detected in regard to the number of evaluative devices produced (Capps et al., 2000). The children with autism and the children with developmental delays did, however, use a significantly more limited range of evaluative devices when compared to typically developing children (Capps et al., 2000). To establish whether there were any discrepancies in performance as a result of the task, two methods were included: telling a personal narrative and generating a story. The former involved participants engaging in a semi-structured conversation with the examiner whereas the story generation task involved using a wordless picture book. Overall, the typically developing children produced longer stories, used more complex syntax, and made significantly more causal attributions about affective and cognitive states compared to children with autism and the children with developmental delays who did not differ from one another (Capps et al., 2000). The children with autism and the children with developmental delays tended to label emotions and they focused more upon the actions or behaviours of characters when producing causal attributions (Capps et al., 2000). Characters actions are observable whereas mental states must be inferred. It must be noted that the children with autism, developmental delays, and the typically developing children were all matched according to language abilities using the Clinical Evaluation of Language Fundamentals (CELF, Semel et al., 1987). These findings provide support to the claim that narrative procedures are sensitive enough to be able to detect discrepancies between groups which standardised clinical assessments may not be able to pick up on. The advantage of matching participants according to language abilities is that it provides a means of assessing for any discrepancies in narrative performance which cannot be accounted for by these measures. There are, however, some limitations of the study which must be addressed. Firstly, the sample size was small as 13 children with autism, 13 children with developmental delays, and 13 typically developing children participated in the study (Capps et al., 2000, p. 193). Nevertheless, the difficulties faced by researchers in being able to recruit willing participants, particularly amongst clinical populations, should not be underestimated. The methodological procedure used in the study may have also impacted upon the sample size; the researchers translated audio recordings, which is a time-consuming task, therefore it may not have been possible to recruit a significantly larger sample due to time constraints. Secondly, the intelligent quotient and mental age scores were not obtained for the typically developing children therefore it is not possible to draw comparisons between all three groups in regard to this. The typically developing children were also excluded from partaking in the false-belief tasks despite the children with autism and the children with developmental delays undertaking these assessments. Thirdly, the results from the two narrative methods were used collectively therefore it cannot be distinguished whether there were any discrepancies between the use of syntactic and evaluative devices employed in the personal and storybook narrative procedures.

5.3.1 Narratives in relation to Theory of Mind

Narrative procedures have been used in conjunction with false-belief tasks in prior studies and they have proved to be fruitful in eliciting a link between theory of mind and performance on a range of language measures including the number of evaluative devices used (Capps *et al.*, 2000), diversity of evaluation (Capps *et al.*, 2000), internal state language (Capps *et al.*, 2000; Siller *et al.*, 2014), the use of emotion terms (Siller *et al.*, 2014), syntactic diversity (Capps *et al.*, 2000), and the production of complex syntax for children with ASD (Norbury and Bishop, 2003). There is a tendency for mental state terms to occur in sentences which are syntactically complex (Norbury and Bishop, 2003). A study conducted by Farrar *et al.* (2017) found that children with ASD were unable to pass false-belief tasks without having passed both the *say* and *think* complement tasks, whereas typically developing children were able to pass false-belief tasks without passing the complementation tasks. Similarly, Capps *et al.* (2000) reported that narrative abilities were not associated with theory of mind performance for children with developmental delays. There is a link between theory of mind and language abilities (Tager-Flusberg and Sullivan, 1995; Lind and Bowler, 2009; Grazzani *et al.*, 2018), as well as narrative performance in children with ASD (Tager-Flusberg and Sullivan, 1995; Capps *et al.*, 2000).

One of the most well-known tools for assessing theory of mind abilities consists of using false-belief tasks, as previously stated in this book. However, a more advanced measurement of theory of mind abilities involves Happé's (1994) *Strange Stories*. This procedure involves watching a series of vignettes depicting stories including pretence, a lie, white lie, joke, misunderstanding, persuasion, reality, figure of speech, forgetting, double bluff, and contrasting emotions (Losh and Capps, 2003). Individuals are then asked questions based upon the stories and they are then tested on their abilities to comprehend and justify their answers. The stories used are representative of utterances which can occur in everyday social situations (Gillot *et al.*, 2004). With both false-belief tasks and Happe's (1994) *Strange Stories*, there is a certain degree of language comprehension required for a person to be able to understand the demands of theory of mind tasks. For example, participants must be able to understand and respond to questions asked by the researcher. Consequently, individuals with a severe language impairment are often unable to partake as they do not possess the language and/or cognitive skills required to meet the demands.

Previous research has found that children with ASD use significantly less references to emotions compared to typically developing children during storytelling (Losh and Capps, 2003; Siller *et al.*, 2014). In their comprehensive study, Losh and Capps (2003) found that the ability to provide accurate definitions for a range of different emotions was significantly associated with the length of personal and storybook narratives, the frequency and diversity of complex syntax, and evaluative devices for children with autism or AS. The study provides some important insights into the relation between language, emotion, and narrative performance. There were three different categories of emotions investigated: these were simple, complex, and complex, self-conscious emotions. Simple emotions consisted of happy, sad, angry, afraid, and disgusted. Complex emotions consisted of curious, disappointed, and surprised. Complex, self-conscious emotions consisted of proud, embarrassed, guilty, and ashamed. The ability to provide accurate definitions for a range of emotions was significantly associated with the frequency of mental state language in both narrative procedures, and with the frequency of causal language in the personal narrative context for children with autism or AS (Losh and Capps, 2003, p. 247). The wordless picture book *Frog Where Are You?* (1969), created by Mercer Mayer, was used for the storybook procedure. Most researchers investigating narrative performance using wordless picture books have utilised Mayer's collection as they have become well-established within narrative studies. The story *Frog, Where Are You?* is about a boy and his dog embarking upon a journey to find his pet frog, who had escaped from a jar in the boy's home and gone missing. There are a range of simple emotions depicted in the story, such as surprise when the boy found out his pet frog was missing, anger when he noticed that his dog smashed the frogs jar whilst jumping out of a window, and happiness when he eventually found his pet frog in a pond. According to the basic theory of emotion, there are six universal states: anger, disgust, enjoyment, fear, sadness, and surprise (Ekman, no date). Each of these states can be depicted through the use of distinguishable facial expressions. For example, facial expressions characteristic of surprise consists of raising the eyebrows and upper eyelids, and the jaw positioned downwards (Ekman, no date).

Evaluative devices are an important part of storytelling and some examples include references to frames of mind, character speech, hedges, negative propositions, and causal statements. A study conducted by Losh and Capps (2003) reported no differences in the use of evaluative devices between the children with autism or AS and the typically developing children when telling a story using the wordless picture book. By contrast, the typically developing children used significantly more evaluative devices than the children with autism or AS during the personal narrative procedure. The children with autism or AS and the typically developing children used more causal statements to explain behaviour than references to thoughts and emotions in Losh and Capps' (2003) study, although there were notable differences between the two groups. The typically developing children produced significantly more causal statements overall during both narrative procedures. Meanwhile, the children with autism or AS used significantly fewer explanations in reference to causes of internal states and behaviour during both narrative contexts (Losh and Capps, 2003). This is in line with other studies which have found that children with ASD do not use internal state language as frequently as their typically developing peers (Siller *et al.*, 2014), and they may provide fewer appropriate explanations in reference to characters internal states (Tager-Flusberg and Sullivan, 1995). To establish whether there were any notable differences in regard to emotions, children were assessed on their ability to provide accurate definitions for a range of different emotions. Losh and Capps (2003) found that the children with autism or AS provided significantly fewer accurate definitions for a range of simple, complex, and complex, self-conscious emotions compared to typically developing children. Although the study yields interesting findings, there are some limitations which must be considered. Firstly, Losh and Capps (2003) did not distinguish between the three different sub-types of emotions as the results were used collectively. Thus, it is not possible to establish whether the children with autism or AS were as proficient as their typically developing peers at being able to define simple emotions, with their difficulties being in defining more complex emotions or whether they were impaired in providing definitions for all three sub-types of emotions. The study would have been more insightful if distinctions were provided, considering that the children with autism or AS were also impaired in their ability to match emotion words with a series of video clips depicting the following five emotions: happiness, sadness, anger, fear, and shame. The video clips were sourced from the Berkeley Empathy Measure.

5.4   Narrative Production in Language Disorder

Previous studies have found that children with SLI produce shorter stories than typically developing children (Kaderavek and Sulzby, 2000; Reilly *et al.*, 2004), make more grammatical tense errors (Norbury and Bishop, 2003), and use a more restricted range of complex syntax (Norbury and Bishop, 2003; Reilly *et al.*, 2004; Blom and Boerma, 2016). Children with SLI have also been found to use a more restricted range and fewer evaluative devices than typically developing children when telling a story (Reilly *et al.*, 2004), as well as use fewer coordinating conjunctions (Kaderavek and Sulzby, 2000). On the other hand, children with SLI were found to use more social engagement devices when telling a story compared to typically developing children (Reilly *et al.*, 2004). Adolescents with SLI were able to produce complex sentences as frequently as typically developing adolescents when telling a story, although they produced more grammatical errors (Wetherell *et al.*, 2007). The type of narrative procedure can influence performance to a certain degree, as previously stated in this book. This is exemplified in a study conducted by Wetherell *et al.* (2007), as they reported that adolescents with SLI and typically developing adolescents produced longer narratives and used more complex syntax when telling a story using a wordless picture book in comparison to telling a personal narrative. This outcome is contrary to that of Losh and Capps (2003) who found children with autism or AS and typically developing children produced longer personal narratives compared to telling a story using a wordless picture book. This discrepancy could be attributed to methodological differences. For example, children were asked a series of questions about a range of topics including family, friends, pets, and hobbies in Losh and Capps' (2003) study whereas adolescents were instructed to tell a personal narrative about the most annoying person they know in Wetherell *et al.*'s (2007) study. Thus, there were fewer conversational topics in Wetherell *et al.*'s (2007) study which can account for why adolescents produced longer narratives when telling a story using a wordless picture book.

Most studies measuring narrative performance have focused on a person's use of language. These approaches have failed to address the importance of including any contributing factors, such as prompts and support provided by researchers, which have been essential for the continuation of a narrative. Wetherell *et al.* (2007) found that adolescents with SLI required significantly more prompts and support than their typically developing peers during the production of spontaneous narratives and during a storytelling task using a wordless picture book. During the spontaneous narrative task, the researcher signalled that they were paying attention by nodding their head and responding with *uh huh* (Wetherell *et al.*, 2007, p. 591). It is worth highlighting that *uh huh* is an example of a phatic interjection, however this topic will be explored in more detail in the following chapter. The researcher's input was also noted if they expressed empathy, reassurance, or agreement, and their utterances were classed as providing support if it was fundamental to the participants continuation of a narrative (Wetherell *et al.*, 2007, p. 592). An example of this would be uttering the emotive interjection *oh dear.* These findings can be used to suggest that *uh huh* and *oh dear* are both interjections which also serve a communicative function. Although the typically developing adolescents did not differ from the adolescents with SLI in regard to the number of fillers produced during the spontaneous narrative task, the latter group produced significantly more fillers when telling a story using a wordless picture book (Wetherell *et al.*, 2007, p. 597). Some examples of fillers include *um, er,* and *you know*. Disfluencies such as repetitions, false starts, and fillers, are often excluded from analyses of narrative performance. Some fillers are also classed as interjections. With this in mind, it can be proposed that interjections provide an insight into a person's linguistic and cognitive abilities as frequent use of fillers may be indicative of difficulties in constructing a linguistic expression.

To date, the number of studies investigating the use of internal state language with individuals diagnosed with a language impairment is extremely limited in scope. On the one hand, prior studies have found that children with SLI reference cognitive states as frequently as their typically developing peers when telling a story, and they are equally as proficient at being able to report on the theme (Norbury and Bishop, 2003; Reilly *et al.*, 2004). Norbury and Bishop (2003) reported that children with SLI are able to use emotion terms as proficiently as typically developing children, as well as children with high-functioning autism and Pragmatic Language Impairment. Emotions are often visibly depicted on characters facial expressions therefore it is possible that this may have aided with the use of emotive terms by all four groups. Most of the children with Pragmatic Language Impairment and high-functioning autism groups were identified as having a language impairment from standardised tests in Norbury and Bishop's (2003) study, highlighting the prevalence of an accompanying language impairment in ASD. Individuals who meet this criterion are sometimes referred to as ASD-LI in the available literature (Williams *et al.*, 2008). Further, Gillot *et al.* (2004) found that children with pho-nologic-syntactic impairments performed similarly to children with autism when they were tested on their theory of mind abilities using Happé's (1994) *Strange Stories*. On the other hand, Manolitsi and Botting (2011) reported that Greek children with SLI were more proficient in being able to reference characters goals and their actions compared to Greek children with ASD as well as produce the content of a story better. The children with SLI and the children with ASD were matched according to expressive language abilities using the Clinical Evaluation of Language Fundamentals: Revised (CELF-R, Semel *et al.*, 1987) or the CELF Preschool edition (CELF-P, Wiig *et al.*, 1992); thus, it cannot account for the notable dis-crepancies in their storytelling abilities. Contrary to this, Norbury *et al.* (2014) reported that children with language impairment produced fewer instances of internal state language when telling a story compared to children with ASD and typically developing children, who did not differ from one another. To date, there are few studies that have investigated theory of mind abilities using individuals with a language impairment and the findings presented thus far are contradictory. Further research into this area is therefore warranted.

Chapter 6.   Interjections

Interjections are defined as linguistic expressions used to express emotion and they can also be used to convey the attitude or mental state of a speaker (Fraser, 1990; Ameka, 1992; Wierzbicka, 1992; Metcalfe *et al.*, 2009; Wharton, 2009; Stange, 2016; Downing and Martínez Caro, 2019). As well as expressing emotions, interjections can be used to fulfil a range of different functions including expressing a person's knowledge, requesting attention, greeting people, and bidding farewell to them (Clark and Fox Tree, 2002). Some examples in English include *aha, psst, hello,* and *goodbye*. Expressions used for the purposes of apologising and thanking others are also classed as interjections (Ameka, 2006).

Interjections are often produced by a speaker in response to certain stimuli or events, thus they are spontaneous vocal expressions (Stange, 2016; Downing and Martínez Caro, 2019). Interjections are typically a part of spoken discourse although they can feature in written texts to create the effect of orality. Also, interjections can be accompanied by facial expressions and gestures (Ameka, 1992; Goddard, 2014). This led to the proposal that interjections are on the cusp of verbal and non-verbal communication as they have been likened to vocal gestures (Ameka, 1992; Asano, 1997). For example, a person may nod their head whilst uttering the phatic interjection *uh-huh* to demonstrate that they are paying attention and have acknowledged a speaker's utterance. By doing so, this may provide encouragement to a speaker.

6.1   Categories of Interjections

6.1.1   *Primary and Secondary Interjections*

At the most basic level, interjections can be sub-divided into primary and secondary forms. Primary interjections are made up of small verbal components or non-words; examples include *oh, ah, um, ooh, wow, ouch* and *uh* (Ameka, 1992; Norrick, 2009). Although primary interjections do not belong to other word classes, they can 'serve as base forms for normal words, such as the verb *to wow* (someone)' (Goddard, 2014, p. 54). The distinction between primary and secondary interjections can be further exemplified through the latter belonging to other word classes, such as nouns and verbs, depending on the semantic meaning (Ameka, 1992; Goddard, 2014). *Boy* is an example of a secondary interjection as it is classed as a noun when used in reference to a male child, although it can be used colloquially to express a range of different emotions including shock, surprise, and excitement (Oxford English Dictionary, 2008). Secondary interjections can also function as intensifiers when they occur in the utterance-initial position; examples include *hell yeah* and *shit no* (Downing and Martínez Caro, 2019). As secondary interjections do not require additional words for an utterance to make sense, they are not elliptical (Ameka, 1992; Wharton, 2009). Secondary interjections also fulfil a discursive function when they are produced in response to another person's utterance or their actions (Downing and Martínez Caro, 2019, p. 93).

Interjections can provide an insight into a speaker's internal mental state, including their emotions and cognition. According to Norrick (2009), primary interjections tend to express information states whereas emotions are primarily conveyed through the use of secondary interjections. Primary interjections are small verbal units which do not contain much semantic meaning compared to secondary interjections. In contrast to Norrick (2009), Dietrich *et al.* (2008) argues that primary interjections convey a speaker's internal state through the use of prosodic cues. In the same vein, Aijmer (2002) asserts that variations made to the intonation, volume, and lengthening of vowels can all provide an insight into a speaker's internal state. This can be illustrated through the primary interjection *ah*, as the elongation of the vowel *a* produced with a high-pitched tone and a rising-falling melody indicates that a speaker is pleased (Dietrich *et al.*, 2008). *Ah* can convey a range of different emotional states including pleasure, surprise, sorrow, and exasperation (Oxford English Dictionary, 2012). Further, *ah* can provide an insight into a speaker's cognitive state when produced as an expression of sudden realisation. Thus, the context must be taken into consideration when formulating an inference about the underlying meaning of a speaker's utterance, exemplifying the relation between interjections and pragmatics.

Like primary interjections, secondary interjections can also provide an insight into a speaker's internal mental state. For example, *God* is a secondary interjection as it classed as a noun when used in reference to a deity, although it can also express a range of emotions including dismay, disgust, and exasperation (Oxford English Dictionary, 2014). *God* also appears in a number of interjectional phrases such as *oh my God*, *thank God*, and *for God's sake*; the aforementioned expressions convey a range of different emotions including surprise, relief, and frustration. Unlike primary interjections, a speaker's internal mental state can be conveyed through the semantic meaning of secondary interjections even if they were uttered in a neutral tone (Dietrich *et al.*, 2008, p. 1751).

Expletives can be subsumed under the classification of secondary interjections as they are defined as profanities exclaimed by a speaker to emphatically fill their speech (Oxford English Dictionary, 2016). To allow for this, expletives must meet the following criteria:

a) They must provide an insight into the speaker's state of mind.
b) They must be uttered spontaneously.
c) They must be able to function as a standalone utterance (Stange, 2016).

Expletives tend to express negative emotions and speakers often produce them with a raised voice (Stange, 2014, p. 14). They can co-occur with the primary interjection *oh*, often used to express a stronger feeling (Aijmer, 2002). *Fuck* is an expletive in English which expresses a range of negative emotions including anger, despair, frustration, and alarm (Oxford English Dictionary, 2008). Similarly, *shit* is another example of an expletive used to express anger, despair, and frustration. However, *shit* can also express excitement which is a positive emotion (Oxford English Dictionary, 2011).

6.1.2   Cognitive, Emotive, Phatic, and Volitive Interjections

Interjections can be sub-divided into several different categories including the expressive, phatic, and volitive (Wierzbicka, 1992; Goddard, 2014). Some interjections can belong to more than one category depending on their function. This will be explored in more detail further on in this chapter. Expressive interjections are defined as vocal gestures used to express a speaker's mental state, although it is worth noting that expressive interjections can be sub-divided into the emotive and cognitive (Ameka, 1992). From this point forward, this paper will not refer to expressive interjections but shall treat emotive and cognitive interjections as two separate entities.

Cognitive interjections convey information states and the knowledge of a person which tend to be related to the time in which an utterance is spoken (Ameka, 1992; Goddard, 2014). *Aha* is an example of a cognitive interjection typically used to express a sudden realisation made (Oxford English Dictionary, 2012). Cognitive and conative interjections are terms which have been used interchangeably throughout previous literature, however for clarification purposes this paper will use the term cognitive from this point forward. Although Stange (2016) acknowledges that both cognitive and emotive interjections can provide an insight into the mental state of a speaker, she argues that they can be distinguished from one-another on the premise that cognitive interjections focus more upon mental processes rather than emotions. More recent attention has focused on treating emotive and cognitive interjections as two entities influential upon one another as a person's thoughts can simultaneously influence their emotions (Goddard, 2014; Downing and Martínez Caro, 2019).

Emotive interjections are used to convey the emotions and sensations that a speaker experiences at a given time; examples include *yuck*, *wow*, *ouch*, and *ugh* (Ameka, 1992).

Phatic interjections play an important role during social interactions as they can be used to maintain social and communicative contact between a speaker and listener (Ameka, 1992). Examples of phatic interjections include the discourse markers *uh-huh* or *mm* and they are often used by a listener to indicate that they are paying attention to a speaker's utterance during spoken discourse. This may prompt the speaker to continue as phatic interjections can provide encouragement (Stange, 2016). This claim can be illustrated through a study conducted by Wetherell *et al.* (2007) who found that adolescents with SLI required significantly more support and encouragement from the researcher, such as through uttering *uh-huh*, when they were tested on their narrative abilities and performance compared to typically developing individuals. As mentioned in the preceding chapter, the study involved participants telling a story in two different formats consisting of using a wordless picture book and producing a personal narrative. The methods chosen in the aforementioned study emphasises the significance of interjections in spoken discourse. The claim that interjections can belong to more than one category can be exemplified through the tendency for phatic interjections to contain a cognitive element as they provide an insight into a speaker's mind (Stange, 2016). For example, *uh huh* is typically used by a speaker to express that they are paying attention, have acknowledged another person's utterance, and they are showcasing their agreement.

Volitive interjections are used to convey a person wanting something in the semantic meaning of their utterance; an example of this would be the English interjection *ssh!* (Wierzbicka, 1992; Goddard, 2014). There is a tendency for a speaker to produce *ssh* in an exclamatory manner as a method of encouraging others to engage in silence. *Ssh* can also be directed towards another person as a signal for them to adjust the loudness of their voice. The close relation between cognitive and volitive interjections can be exemplified through both being used to express a speaker's wants thereby reinforcing the claim that interjections can belong to more than one category. Different theories exist in the literature regarding whether interjections should be classed as being an integral part of language, although this topic will be explored in more depth later on in this chapter. On one hand, Wharton (2009) embodies the argument that interjections are not an integral part of language. Citing the example *ssh*, Wharton (2009) argues that the expression does not convey emotion which is central to the definition of interjections. Despite this, interjections are not restricted to the sole purpose of expressing emotion as they can fulfil a range of functions as previously stated. On the other hand, Stange (2016) asserts that volitive interjections can have an underlying emotive element as a person can become annoyed by the level of noise in the surrounding environment which may prompt them to utter *ssh.*

6.2   Interjections in relation to language

Interjections are universal as they are a part of all languages, however there is great variation among them as they are specific to each language (Asano, 1997; Stange, 2009). Some interjections are found in other languages; for example, the English interjection *hurray* translates to *hurra* in German. The orthography of *hurray* in English shows remarkable similarities to the German translation and the meaning remains unchanged in both languages as it is typically used to express triumph, approval, or provide encouragement (Oxford English Dictionary, 1989).

The study of interjections has largely been neglected as research on the topic is extremely limited in scope (Ameka, 1992; Asano, 1997; Goddard, 2014; Stange, 2016; Downing and Martínez Caro, 2019). There is a growing debate addressing whether interjections are an integral part of language (Ameka, 1992; Wharton, 2009; Stange, 2016). On the one hand, Goffman (1978) argues that interjections should not be classed as a part of language on the premise that they are not standardised words as they do not conform to the conventionalised orthography and phonological rules of a language. While some interjections have a conventionalised orthography, such as *wow* and *yay*, there are deviations in the spelling of some interjections. For example, the Oxford English Dictionary (1989) defines *hum* as an interjection produced by a speaker with their lips closed to indicate hesitation, embarrassment, or dissatisfaction. However, the same interjection is spelled as *hmm* in the Cambridge Dictionary as well as in the Collins and Merriam-Webster dictionaries. The discrepancies in the orthography of some interjections may be problematic for researchers investigating their usage in spoken discourse, particularly when their chosen methodology consists of analysing transcripts from databases as this would require extensive searches.

Some interjections deviate from the phonological rules of a language, although it is not a universal feature (Asano, 1997; Ameka, 1992; Ameka, 2006; Goddard, 2014). The basic structure of a syllable in the English language consists of a vowel which is preceded and/or followed by zero or more segments of consonants (Davenport and Hannahs, 2013, p. 74). For instance, the word *cat* follows the consonant – vowel – consonant structure. Some interjections in English do conform to the vowel and consonant composition of syllable structures and examples include the following: *aw, boo, ew, oh, phew*, and *ugh*. On the other hand, *psst* and *ssh* are two examples of volitive interjections in English which do not conform to the syllable structure as they are composed solely of consonantal segments (Ameka, 2006). Under these conditions, interjections which do not conform to the phonological rules of a language are classed as non-words (Ameka, 2006). The tendency for some interjections to deviate from the phonological rules of a language is one plausible suggestion to explain why the study of interjections has been neglected by linguists to date. Consequently, the number of studies investigating interjections is extremely limited in scope.

There is a tendency for interjections to deviate from the syntactic rules of a language. This is likely to have been another contributing factor in explaining why the topic of interjections has largely been neglected by linguists to date. Wharton (2009) argues that interjections should not be classed as a part of language and they should be treated as two separate entities. Wharton's (2009) claim is based on the premise that interjections are not embedded within the main clause and they are rarely integrated into intonational units. With this in mind, it is important to note that interjections are not uniform, they can function as standalone utterances as they are independent from the syntactic rules governing a language and they are not embedded by the grammar of a clause (Ameka, 1992; Wharton, 2009). On the other hand, the argument that interjections play an important role in language has recently gained traction as they provide an insight into the state of mind of a speaker and their emotions (Asano, 1997; Goddard, 2014; Stange, 2016). The production of interjections by a speaker allows them to express how they are feeling without having to explicitly state their emotions. For example, *yuck* can be used to convey the message *I feel disgusted* and *wow* can be used as a substitute for saying *This is great* (Stange, 2016, p. 7). Thus, it can be proposed that interjections play a crucial role in language development as their ability to function as holophrastic utterances means they are able to express the same communicative content as longer, more complex utterances. There is little published data on interjectional usage with a typically developing cohort. More surprisingly, interjectional usage has not previously been studied amongst individuals with communication disorders. Thus, there is a gap in the literature which this paper strives to address by providing new insights into interjectional usage during storytelling and spontaneous play.

Interjections are often embedded in spoken discourse and they serve an interpersonal function when used in this context (Aijmer, 2002). This may provide an explanation for why some interjections are often classed as discourse markers (Fraser, 1990). Similar to interjections, discourse markers 'are not embedded within the grammar of a clause and they may deviate from the phonological rules of a language' (Fraser, 1990, p. 391). Although Fraser (1990) cites *tsk*, *ahem*, and *ssh* as examples of discourse markers, the paper failed to mention that these are also classed as interjections. This is notable as interjections and discourse markers are often interlinked. Another example of an interjection which simultaneously functions as a discourse marker is *oh*. As it is frequently used during conversational exchanges between interlocutors, *oh* functions as a discourse marker as it serves an interactional purpose (Aijmer, 2002). *Oh* is often produced by a speaker to indicate their acknowledgement and comprehension of another person's utterance and it can also be used as an expression of agreement (Oxford English Dictionary, 2019). Thus, *oh* can provide encouragement as it serves as a backchannelling device, indicating that a listener is paying attention to a speaker's utterance (Aijmer, 2002). According to Aijmer (2002), *oh* occurs most commonly after statements as well as during verbal exchanges which follow a question-and-answer format. There are, however, many different uses for the word *oh* which must be considered. For example, a speaker may produce *oh* upon realising they have made an error therefore it can signal they intend to correct themself (Aijmer, 2002). When *oh* is produced with a falling tone, it often signals a speaker's acknowledgement of new information (Aijmer, 2002). Additionally, *oh* can be used to introduce an utterance expressing a speaker's sudden recollection which may be accompanied by a succeeding utterance. Bolinger (1989) provides insightful commentary upon the use of *oh* being used to save face as a speaker may utter this interjection instead of being confrontational. In this respect, *oh* expresses a speaker's doubt or disagreement with a previous utterance made. Together, these findings reinforce the claim that interjections function as pragmatic markers as context must be taken into consideration when trying to formulate an inference about the meaning of a speaker's interjectional use and any accompanying utterances (Downing and Martinez Caro, 2019). Thus far, the discursive function of *oh* has been addressed although it is important to note that it can also express a range of different emotions including surprise, frustration, disappointment, sorrow, and relief (Oxford English Dictionary, 2019). Prosodic cues are vital in distinguishing between the different uses of *oh* as variations made in a speaker's pitch differentiates expressing dismay and joy (Stange, 2016, p. 22). For example, if *oh* was uttered by a speaker with a high pitch then it can be used to convey either joy or surprise. By contrast, *oh* produced with a low pitch expresses dismay or sorrow. According to Aijmer (2002), *oh* is one of the most frequently used words in the London-Lund corpus; this is a composition of fifty direct conversations between British adults from 1961 until 1976, most of whom were academics. Despite this, Stange (2016) was unable to conduct an analysis on *oh* as the London-Lund corpus did not contain any prosodic information therefore its uses could not be decoded. This is a major disadvantage of using transcripts to analyse interjectional usage.

Irony is defined as the use of language to express the opposite meaning of a speaker's utterance (Oxford English Dictionary, 2013). Irony can create a humorous effect or add emphasis to a speaker's utterance. A speaker can use interjections to express irony; for example, a student uttering *yay* upon finding out that they had failed an exam they had recently undertaken. Considering that a student is likely to feel disappointed in the event of this happening, *yay* contradicts the literal, semantic meaning as it is an interjection typically used to express triumph. This illustrates that the intended meaning of a speaker's utterance cannot always correctly be deciphered when it is taken at face value, exemplifying the context dependency of interjections. Some individuals with ASD have difficulties in understanding and interpreting emotional expressions (Hobson, 1986). The ability to comprehend ironic expressions involves a person being able to understand other people's minds as well as complex emotions (Pexman *et al.*, 2011). Stange (2016) argues that interjections lose their character, by definition, when used to convey irony as it does not express a true representation of a speaker's internal mental state. On the other hand, it can be argued that interjections used to convey irony signify a speaker's internal state although it is not explicit. Advanced cognitive skills are required as the listener must detect that the underlying meaning of the speaker's utterance signifies the opposite of what was said, allowing for the attribution of an appropriate mental state. The ability to process unintentional acts is more cognitively demanding than those which are deliberate, although an understanding of both is crucial to understanding human behaviour (Rosset and Rottman, 2014). A study conducted by Pexman *et al.* (2011) found that high-functioning children with autism were able to detect a speaker's use of irony, however they were not as proficient as typically developing children in being able to detect intentional humour embedded in ironic expressions. This finding is noteworthy considering that ironic expressions are primarily used to create a humorous effect, often used in social situations. Thus, children with high-functioning autism may find it difficult to navigate social situations when irony is used. To date, there are no published studies investigating whether children with ASD are as proficient as typically developing children at being able to recognise a speaker's intentions using interjections. This may be a fruitful area of research considering that inter-jections can be used to express cognitive and emotional states as well as convey irony. Con-sidering that pragmatics is a universal impairment in ASD, further research into interjectional usage may yield new insights into whether individuals with ASD find it difficult to understand and interpret the meaning of interjections as they are bound by context.

As well as context, prosody can be influential in determining the meaning of an interjection. In a preliminary study, Dietrich *et al.* (2008) investigated regions of the brain activated upon hearing the expression of interjections. The study consisted of 12 typically developing adults, all of whom were right-handed, who underwent functional magnetic resonance imaging (fMRI) as they listened to twelve different German interjections uttered in affective and neutral tones (Dietrich *et al.*, 2008, p. 1751). Functional magnetic resonance imaging (fMRI) is a non-invasive technique used to measure changes in blood oxygenation and its flow which occur in response to neural activity. When there is an increase in neuronal activity, there is simul-taneously an increase in demand for oxygen to certain regions of the brain (Devlin, no date). Thus, fMRI is able to detect which parts of the brain are activated when certain cognitive tasks are carried out (National Health Service, 2019). There were twelve interjections chosen for investigation, equally divided into high-lexical and low-lexical utterances. High-lexical inter-jections are associated with an explicit semantic meaning and this group consisted of the following: *hurra* (hurray), *pfui* (ugh), *heda*, *oha*, *oje* (oh dear) and *achje* (oh man). By contrast, low-lexical interjections consisted of vowels occurring in isolation therefore they were not associated with a particular semantic meaning and this group consisted of the following: *a*, *pah*, *ja* (yes), *e*, *ach* and *o* (oh). The distinction between high and low-lexical interjections can be further exemplified through reliance on prosody to convey meaning. When a high-lexical interjection is uttered by a speaker in a neutral tone, emotion can still be conveyed through its semantic meaning. This is not the case for low-lexical interjections as they are dependent on prosody to convey emotion (Dietrich *et al.*, 2008). During the study, participants listened to each group of interjections uttered by a speaker in an affective and neutral tone. One significant finding consisted of the bilateral hemodynamic activation of the superior temporal cortex, elicited while participants listened to all four categories of interjections differing in prosody and lexical load (Dietrich *et al.*, 2008, p. 1754). The superior temporal gyrus plays a fundamental part in auditory perception and speech, and it encompasses Wernicke's area (Clark *et al.*, 2018). Together, these findings support the claim that the superior temporal gyrus is one region of the brain associated with emotion recognition. Dietrich *et al.* (2008, p. 1754) states that 'the responses to affective prosody and emotional lexicality showed a nearly complete overlap with the rostral parts of the supra-temporal plane, including primary auditory areas. In contrast, a clear-cut scissor-like divergence in medio-lateral direction could be documented at a more caudal level: the activation pattern associated with prosody encroached upon the posterior insula, the responses to lexicality, by contrast, extended from lateral parts of the supra-temporal plane into the superior temporal sulcus and middle temporal gyrus.' These findings reveal that different regions of the brain are activated when processing high and low-lexical interjections, which may be in part due to the processing of prosodic information encoded in low-level interjections.

6.2.1 *The Acquisition and Use of Interjections*

Interjections need to be acquired by a speaker and they are a significant part of language, exemplified through some interjections being amongst the first words acquired by an infant as well as their ability to function as holophrastic utterances. As previously stated in chapter four, infants begin to produce cooing sounds such as *uoh* and *aah* within the first six months (National Health Service, no date). Interjections play an important role in early language development as they allow for a speaker to communicate their mental states without necessarily having fully mastered the syntactic, phonological, morphological, semantic, and pragmatic rules underpinning a language. The comprehension of language typically precedes production therefore it can be suggested that some children may be able to understand the meaning of some interjections before they acquire the phonological skills required to be able to produce them (Stange, 2016). This can be exemplified in a study conducted by Fenson *et al.* (1994, pp. 92-93) who found that some infants demonstrated comprehension of the interjection *uh oh* by 10 months although they were not able to produce it until 14 months old. However, some children may acquire interjections at an earlier or a later stage as the development of language is variable and language acquisition is subject to fluctuation, particularly during the initial stages of a person's life. Additionally, some infants were able to comprehend the interjection *yum yum* at 10 months old although they were not able to produce it until 16 months old (Fenson *et al.*, 1994, pp. 92-93). These findings confirm that interjections are among the first words acquired by infants, giving scope to the argument that interjections are an integral part of language. Phonological features may also influence the production of some interjections (Asano, 1997; Stange, 2016). For example, *goodness me* and *upsidaisy* are more complex than *oh* and *ow*. Thus, children are more likely to produce the former interjections at a later stage once they have grasped the phonological skills to be able to do so. Also, *upsidaisy* is an interjection typically uttered by adults to children to encourage them to stand up after falling, for example, or if they have made a minor mistake. It is needless to say that children may utter this interjection when imitating adults as they undergo language development.

Interjections play an important part in early language acquisition as they can function as one-word holophrastic utterances therefore they are able to express an entire phrase or a combination of ideas through a single word. Also, interjections play an important role during interactions between children and adults (Goddard, 2014; Stange, 2016). This may be in part due to the communicative efficiency of interjections as they are capable of conveying the same message as longer utterances. Adults can also teach children not to do things through using interjections (Stange, 2016). For example, an adult may express alarm by uttering *no* with a raised voice upon seeing a child put an inedible object into their mouth which has the potential to cause harm. Thus, a child may learn to establish a connection between the meaning of the interjection *no* and their actions or behaviour.

Previous studies investigating interjections have based their findings upon analyses of transcripts of spoken discourse. There are some advantages to using this methodological procedure which must be considered. Interjections are a part of spoken discourse therefore there is the possibility that transcripts may contain an abundance of interjections (Goddard, 2014). Transcripts also contain samples of language produced naturally which gives rise to the possibility that speakers may have produced interjections in an authentic manner (Goddard, 2014). Using transcripts obtained from the Child Language Data Exchange System (CHILDES), Asano (1997) conducted an investigation into the acquisition and usage of the interjections *ouch, yuck,* and *oops*. There were three different types of data sets included: 52 sets of recorded speech produced by one female child between the ages of 1 year 11 months and 3 years 3 months, 21 sets of recorded speech of three female children aged between 11 months and 2 years 11 months during mother-child interactions, and 67 sets of recorded speech of twenty-four children aged between 2 years 1 month and 5 years 2 months during parent-child interactions (Asano, 1997, p. 4). All children were in the process of learning American English. Asano (1997, p. 5) reported that the earliest usage of the interjection *yuck* was produced by a child aged 1 year 10 months whereas *oops* was first uttered by a child aged 2 years and *ouch* by a child aged 2 years 1 month in reference to their own pain. Imaginary pain was initially produced by a child aged 2 years 10 months during pretend play while *ouch* was extended to express pain experienced by another person or object at the same age (Asano, 1997, pp. 5-6). These findings suggest that emotive interjections are among the earliest to be acquired. It is possible to hypothesise that phatic interjections may be acquired at a later stage of development once children have grasped the linguistic and communicative abilities required to interact with others. No previous study has investigated the order in which interjections are typically acquired therefore this could be a fruitful topic for further research. The study conducted by Asano (1997) was influential in encouraging Stange (2016) to conduct further research into the acquisition and use of interjections. Similar to Asano (1997), the findings from Stange's (2016) study were based upon analyses of transcripts of spoken discourse obtained from the CHILDES. This included 804 recording files of 12 children aged between 1 year 8 months and 3 years old during play sessions (Stange, 2016, p. 76). Data was also obtained from the British National Corpus which consisted of transcripts of spoken discourse between adult interlocutors (Stange, 2016). Collectively, these studies are fruitful in providing an insight into the acquisition and use of interjections predominantly by children. Despite this, interjectional usage among adolescents remains to be investigated. This paper strives to address this gap in the literature by including both children and adolescents in the study.

6.3 Interjections in relation to Theory of Mind

Theory of mind involves the ability to recognise and understand one's own mental states as well as attribute these to others. Emotions are a mental state therefore the ability to comprehend and recognise that another person can have a different emotional state to oneself is a fundamental part of theory of mind. Previous studies have found that the ability to perceive emotions can be difficult for some individuals with ASD (Thaler *et al.*, 2018). One of the most well-known methods used to assess emotion recognition involves asking a person to formulate an interpretation about another person's emotional state, often based upon facial expressions. It is now well established that theory of mind is an impairment in ASD. However, the most well-known tools for assessing theory of mind abilities include false-belief tasks and Happe's (1994) *Strange Stories*, both of which require individuals to

63

have a certain degree of linguistic proficiency to be able to meet the demands of the task. With this in mind, it might be worth using a different method in future investigations whereby participants are assessed on their theory of mind abilities through using interjections. There is the potential that it may yield interesting findings considering that interjections can provide an insight into a person's internal mental state including cognition and emotion. This is an important issue for future research given that a large proportion of the autistic population, who have an accompanying language impairment or other co-occurring neurological disorder, are often omitted from research. There is a tendency for researchers to recruit individuals with ASD whose language and intellectual abilities are classed as being within the normal range, although this may be to ensure that tasks are accessible for participants. Interjections, however, are independent from the syntactic rules governing a language and they are not embedded by the grammar of a clause. Interjections also play an important role in early language development as they allow for a speaker to communicate their mental states without necessarily having fully mastered the syntactic, phonological, morphological, semantic, and pragmatic rules underpinning a language. Thus, the intrinsic link between interjectional usage, linguistic abilities, and theory of mind remains to be explored.

According to the Oxford English Dictionary (2004), the production of *ouch* in response to someone else's pain is an expression of empathy. The terms sympathy and empathy are often used interchangeably, however there are subtle differences in their semantic meaning which must be addressed. Sympathy refers to the state of being affected by the condition of another person which may cause them to feel a similar emotion (Oxford English Dictionary, 1989). The term empathy is defined as the ability to identify and understand another person's thoughts, feelings, and emotions (Baron-Cohen, 2002). Although both demonstrate the acknowledgement of another person's emotions, the distinction between them lays in a person feeling affected by the condition of another person with sympathy whereas this is not the case with empathy (Chismar, 1988). There are a number of interjections which express empathy including *aw, oh dear*, and *goodness gracious*. Children with ASD can use interjections to express their own internal mental states as well as express empathy towards others. This can be illustrated through a primary example of an observation I made whereby a child with ASD, Jack, uttered the interjection *Oh no!* upon realising that he made an error in his mathematics work.

Jack: *Oh no! I put 12 [seconds] instead of 19!*

Mary: *Oh dear! That's okay.*

Jack's utterance prompted Mary, a child with ASD, to utter *Oh dear!* in response. *Oh dear* is an interjection used to express a range of different feeling states including surprise, anxiousness, distress, regret, or sympathy (Oxford English Dictionary, 1989). Taking the context into consideration, it can be plausibly suggested that Mary's use of the interjection *oh dear* was an exclamation of empathy towards Jack as she was able to recognise his disappointment upon being informed by the classroom teacher that he wrote down an incorrect answer to one of the questions. This interpretation can be reinforced through Mary's succeeding utterance of saying *That's okay*, intended to provide reassurance to Jack.

Empathy and theory of mind often work in conjunction with one-another and they are both required in complex social situations (Premack and Woodruff, 1978; Preckel *et al.*, 2018). Their interrelation can be exemplified further as empathy and theory of mind activate shared parts of the brain (Ibanez *et al.*, 2013). Empathy can help with understanding another person's mental state, formulate predictions about other people's behaviour, and promote social behaviour and interactions (Mestre *et al.*, 2009). This led to Baron-Cohen (2002, p. 248) proposing that empathy is the 'most powerful way of understanding and predicting the social world.' Thus, empathy and theory of mind abilities are both fundamental components of human communication. The ability to empathise and systemise is applicable to every human being although one may be more developed than the other. According to Baron-Cohen's (2002) proposal of the extreme-male brain theory of autism, the male brain is wired for systemising being more developed than empathising. The latter involves the ability to attribute mental states to others as well provide an appropriate response to another person's affective state (Baron-Cohen, 2002, p. 248). On the other hand, systemising involves 'the drive to analyse the variables in a system to derive the underlying rules that govern the behaviour of a system' (Baron-Cohen, 2002, p. 248). However, systemising cannot predict sudden changes made in a person's behaviour (Baron-Cohen, 2002). According to Baron-Cohen's (2002) theory, individuals who are more developed in empathising than systemising have a female brain. However, biological sex does not determine whether a person has a male or a female brain. For example, some females may be more developed in systemising than empathising therefore they present with the male brain type (Baron-Cohen, 2002). On the other hand, some males may favour empathising over systemising therefore they present with the female brain type (Baron-Cohen,

2002). The balanced brain is a term used if an individual denotes equal measures of systemising and empathising (Baron-Cohen, 2002). There are several studies that can be used to support Baron-Cohen's (2002) extreme male-brain theory of autism. For example, Happé (1995) found that 25 per cent of female participants with autism passed a theory of mind task compared to 19 per cent of male participants with autism. However, the results should be interpreted with caution as there was a discrepancy between the number of participants recruited and their biological sex. This can be illustrated through there being 54 males with autism who partook in Happé's (1995, p. 848) study whereas there were only 16 females with autism. Thus, participants were not matched accordingly based upon biological sex. Considering that males are four times more likely to receive a diagnosis of ASD compared to females, it is possible that it may have been more difficult to recruit females with ASD to partake in the study (American Psychiatric Association, 2013).

6.4   The Different Uses of Oops

Response cries are defined as being inadvertent exclamatory interjections produced by a speaker (Goffman, 1978). Response cries can be sub-divided according to the following: transition displays, spill cries, threat startles, revulsion sounds, strain grunts, pain cries, floor cues, sexual moans, and audible glees (Goffman, 1978). According to Goffman (1978), response cries are not fully-fledged words as they do not express a linguistic statement. However, it can be argued that some response cries do express a linguistic statement. For example, the spill cry *oops* can be used to convey the message *I didn't mean to do that* when used as an expression of surprise or apologising. Thus, spill cries are able to convey the same communicative content as longer, more complex utterances. With this in mind, it can be suggested that individuals with limited expressive language abilities produce interjections as holophrastic utterances more often than individuals with normal language skills. A primary example of an observation I made consisted of a child with ASD uttering *oops* upon realising that he switched the classroom lights on before a short video clip had finished playing. Taking the context into consideration, it can be inferred that *oops* served as a cognitive interjection as he realised that he had made an error; this prompted him to switch the classroom lights back on until the teacher instructed him to turn them off. The pupil with autism had extremely limited expressive language abilities, having observed him using a maximum of three-word utterances such as *I want biscuit*. Thus, the significance of interjections should not be underestimated as they play an important role in language development as they are able to convey information about the mental state of a speaker without the linguistic complexity of a fully-fledged utterance.

Children can produce *oops* by the age of 1 year 7 months (Asano, 1997, p. 8). Although Goffman (1978) argues that response cries are not fully-fledged words, he does acknowledge that *oops* conforms to the phonological rules of a language as it consists of the vowel and consonantal composition of syllables in English. Furthermore, Goffman (1978) proposes that response cries do not have a discursive function as they do not necessarily address another person. Conversely, it can be suggested that spill cries can sometimes lead to a communicative exchange. For example, a person may utter *oops* after falling over which may prompt another person to approach them therefore there is the potential for a communicative exchange. In the same vein, Stange (2016) claims that spill cries can function as warning signals when they are uttered in the presence of other people. The meaning of an interjection is dependent on the context in which it was uttered. For example, *oops* tends to be uttered by a speaker upon realising that they have made a mistake albeit a minor one (Goffman, 1978; Stange, 2016). In the event of *oops* being uttered when a serious mistake has been made, the interjection may be perceived as being ironic or a speaker having misjudged a situation (Stange, 2016, p. 62). Thus, a speaker must be able to distinguish between a minor and a major mistake to produce *oops* in a context that is deemed appropriate (Stange, 2016). This concerns pragmatics.

6.5   Should fillers be classed as an interjection?

Spoken language is not a continuous form as speakers require time to process and formulate utterances. Disfluencies such as false starts, repetitions, and fillers are common in discursive contexts. Fillers are sounds or words produced by a speaker to indicate a pause or hesitation during discourse. Comprehension of a speaker's utterance can be delivered through fillers and they can also be used to communicate information (Irvine *et al.*, 2016). Additionally, fillers can indicate that a person's attention has waned (Goffman, 1978). Fillers tend to occur in the utterance-initial position most often, signalling a delay in speaking (Clark and Fox Tree, 2002; O'Connell and Kowal, 2005; Irvine *et al.*, 2016). Nevertheless, fillers are not restricted to the utterance-initial position as they can be embedded within an utterance.

Different theories exist in the literature regarding whether fillers should be classed as an integral part of language. On the one hand, Goffman (1978) argues that verbalisations produced by a speaker to fill pauses such as *ah*, *uh*, and *um* should be classed as non-words as they have a similar function to response cries. On the other hand, the argument that fillers are deserving of classification as English words was given further traction through their conformity to the syntactic and prosodic rules which govern language (Clark and Fox Tree, 2002). Additionally, fillers are a universal feature of language which communicate information about discourse therefore they are an integral part of language (Irvine *et al.*, 2016). This can be exemplified through the fillers *uh* and *um* having been used most frequently during conversational activities in Gorman *et al.*'s (2016) study, occurring in the utterance-initial position most often thereby highlighting their discursive function. It is worth highlighting that *uh* and *um* are both examples of fillers which are also classed as primary interjections, providing an insight into a speaker's cognitive state. There is a tendency for researchers investigating narrative abilities to omit disfluencies, such as fillers and repetitions, from analyses of linguistic expressions produced by a speaker. Disfluencies, however, provide an insight into a speaker's narrative, cognitive, and linguistic abilities and should therefore be included in future research. For example, frequent use of fillers during spoken discourse can be used to indicate a speaker's difficulty in processing information or formulating an utterance.

6.5.1 The Use of Fillers in Autism Spectrum Disorder and Specific Language Impairment

Gorman *et al.* (2016) found that there were significant differences in the frequency of the filler *um* used among children with ASD, SLI, and typically developing children. Although *um* is used to indicate hesitation, it can also be uttered by a speaker to indicate agreement (Oxford English Dictionary, 1989). *Um* accounted for more than 70 per cent of the total number of fillers used by the children with SLI and the typically developing children (Gorman *et al.*, 2016, p. 862). Moreover, *um* accounted for approximately 40 per cent of the total number of fillers used by children with ASD (Gorman *et al.*, 2016, p. 862). Although there were no significant differences reported in the frequency of the filler *uh-um* used by the typically developing children and the children with SLI, the filler was used considerably less by the children with ASD (Gorman *et al.*, 2016). It is worth noting that *uh-um* is often used to indicate agreement therefore it functions as a backchannelling device. *Uh-um* is also classed as a phatic inter-jection, used to provide encouragement to a speaker during discourse. No significant differences were reported in the use of the filler *uh* among the three groups, although its contextual uses are restricted to solely expressing hesitation (Oxford English Dictionary, 1989). According to Clark and Fox Tree (2002), *uh* is used to indicate that there will be a minor delay in speaking whereas *um* suggests a major delay in speaking during spontaneous speech. The London-Lund corpus was used in Clark and Fox Tree's (2002, p. 80) analysis of *uh* and *um*; this is a composition of fifty direct conversations between British adults from 1961 until 1976, most of whom were academics. Thus, the transcripts are not entirely representative of fillers used in everyday life and the findings may not be applicable to some. Referring back to Gorman *et al.*'s (2016) study, the data obtained was based on recorded sessions using the Autism Diagnostic Observation Schedule (ADOS, Lord *et al.*, 2000) which is a semi-structured, standardised assessment of social interaction, communication, and play. The ADOS (Lord *et al.*, 2000) is conducted by trained clinicians and it is used to assess and diagnose autism and other pervasive developmental disorders. The sessions were composed of four different activities which included make believe and joint interactive play, describing a picture, telling a story from a book, and conversation. All the children were administered the ADOS (Lord *et al.*, 2000) and the sessions were later transcribed. Although Gorman *et al.*'s (2016) study provides an insight into the comparative use of fillers by children with ASD and SLI compared to typically developing children, there are some limitations which must be addressed. Firstly, Gorman *et al.* (2016) did not distinguish between the contextual uses in which *um* was uttered by each speaker therefore it is not apparent whether the typically developing children and the children with SLI used *um* to signal agreement more frequently than indicating a delay in speaking. Secondly, there were significantly more children with ASD recruited to take part in the study compared to children with SLI; there were 50 children with ASD, 43 typically developing children, and 17 children with SLI (Gorman *et al.*, 2016, p. 857). There were also significantly more male participants than females as 45 out of 50 children with ASD were male, 31 out of 43 typically developing children were male, and 11 out of 17 children with SLI were male (Gorman *et al.*, 2016, p. 857). The biological sex ratio is representative of the higher prevalence of ASD and SLI in males in comparison to females. For example, males are four times more likely to receive a diagnosis of ASD compared to females (American Psychiatric Association, 2013; Baio *et al.*, 2018). Although the DSM-5 (American Psychiatric Association, 2013) does not evidence the prevalence of language disorder in relation to biological sex, studies have reported that a diagnosis of language disorder is more prevalent in males than females (Stromswold, 1998). The interrelation between autism and language disorder can be exemplified through Gorman *et al.*'s (2016, p. 856) study as 25 out of the 50 children with

ASD were identified as having an accompanying language impairment. All of the participants included in the aforementioned study were classed as high functioning as they had a full-scale intelligence quotient score of 70 or above. With this in mind, the study might have been more insightful if the researchers included individuals with ASD whose intelligent quotient scores were below 70. By doing so, this would have provided a more representative sample considering that the variation of intellectual functioning in ASD is vast. This can be demonstrated through Charman *et al.*'s (2011, p. 621) study investigating the intelligent quotient (IQ) scores of 100 adolescents with ASD, having reported that 55.2 per cent of individuals were identified as having an intellectual disability as their IQ scores were below 70. Moreover, 16.6 per cent of participants had a below average IQ score of between 70-84, 25.4 per cent of participants had an average IQ score of between 85-114, and 2.7 per cent of participants had an above average IQ score of above 115 (Charman *et al.*, 2011, p. 621). These findings reveal that the large majority of individuals with ASD, who took part in the study, had an intellectual disability.

The use of fillers was investigated in a recent study conducted by Irvine *et al.* (2016) who found that individuals with ASD produced significantly fewer *ums* than typically developing individuals and individuals with optimal outcome. This is in line with Gorman *et al.*'s (2016) findings. ASD is regarded as a lifelong condition, however a small minority of individuals diagnosed with the disorder have been found to no longer meet the criteria for ASD in follow-up assessments (Fein *et al.*, 2013). The term optimal outcome is given to individuals who no longer present with the symptoms required for a diagnosis of ASD and their intellectual functioning is within the normal range (Fein *et al.*, 2013). There were no group differences reported in the production of the filler *uh* by the individuals with ASD, optimal outcome, and typically developing individuals (Irvine *et al.*, 2016). These findings are in line with Gorman *et al.*'s (2016) results. Nevertheless, an association was reported between the severity of ASD and the use of the filler *um* (Irvine *et al.*, 2016). The production of the filler *um* was not associated with the executive functions or general language deficits of the individuals with ASD (Irvine *et al.*, 2016). This indicates that *um* is characteristic of the social deficits in ASD as the filler serves a communicative function (Irvine *et al.*, 2016). Furthermore, the outcome of the study can be used to suggest that when *uh* is used as a filler, it serves the needs of a speaker as it provides time for them to process an utterance whereas the filler *um* is beneficial to a listener as it can be used to show agreement. To summarise, children with ASD have been found to produce the filler *um* less frequently than children with SLI, typically developing children, and children with optimal outcome. Similarly, children with ASD produced *uh-um* significantly less than children with SLI and typically developing children (Gorman *et al.*, 2016). *Um* and *uh-um* are both fillers used to indicate agreement. Interestingly, an association was detected between the use of the filler *um* and the severity of ASD in Irvine *et al.*'s (2016) study. Children with ASD did not differ from children with SLI and typically developing children in their use of the filler *uh*, although it is worth noting that this filler indicates hesitation (Gorman *et al.*, 2016; Irvine *et al.*, 2016).

6.6   Limitations of Previous Studies

Spoken dialogue is the most natural form of conversation and interjections appear in the most natural use of language. Previous studies investigating the acquisition and use of interjections have based their findings upon analyses of transcripts of spoken discourse obtained from an online database. For example, Asano's (1997, p. 4) study was based on recordings from twenty-eight children, aged between 11 months and 5 years 2 months, during parent-child interactions. Stange's (2016, p. 76) study was based on transcripts of spoken discourse of twelve children aged between 1 year 8 months and 3 years old during play sessions. Thus, prior studies have concentrated on children whereas interjectional usage among adolescents remains to be investigated. This paper strives to address this gap in the literature by incorporating both children and adolescents in the study. Also, there is the possibility that interjections may have been omitted from some transcripts by researchers who may not have deemed them to be an integral part of language (Stange, 2016). Throughout this book, it has been argued that interjections are a fundamental part of language; this can be exemplified through interjections being among the first words acquired by children. The findings from this study provide further support to this argument, which shall be explored in greater detail in the following chapters. To date, no previous study has investigated the use of interjections among individuals with a neurodevelopmental disorder. This preliminary study is the first to do so, and this paper aims to address gaps in the literature by incorporating children and adolescents with ASD, ASD-LI, and DLD alongside a typically developing cohort. There is the possibility that the results from this study will pave the way for further research into interjectional usage, including among clinical populations.

6.7   Summary of the literature review

During social interactions, interlocutors may express how they are feeling to other people. Emotion recognition involves forming an interpretation about another person's emotional state; this can be achieved through taking a range of factors into account such as facial expressions, gestures, body language, and vocal cues. To date, emotion recognition has been the primary focus of research whereas emotional expression warrants further investigation. The current study strives to address this issue through conducting an investigation into the use of interjections by children and adolescents with ASD, ASD-LI, and DLD in comparison to a typically developing cohort. By definition, interjections are utterances used to express emotion and they can also be used to convey the attitude or mental state of a speaker. Internal mental states are composed of a person's knowledge, beliefs, feelings, intentions, and desires. The ability to attribute mental states to other people is a social-cognitive skill which can help to predict and explain the behaviour and actions of other people, a concept known as theory of mind. As well as expressing mental states, interjections can be used to fulfil a range of different functions including expressing a person's knowledge, requesting attention, greeting people, and bidding farewell to them.

Interjections can be categorised according to the following: cognitive, emotive, phatic, and volitive. **Cognitive interjections** convey information states and the knowledge of a person which tend to be related to the time in which an utterance is spoken. Narratives can provide an insight into a person's cognitive abilities as the internal states of characters may not be explicit; the narrator, therefore, must be able to connect elements of the story together cohesively and draw inferences to create a story which has meaning (Norbury and Bishop, 2003). In the present study, a narrative task was included to see whether speakers were able to express characters internal states through the use of cognitive interjections. The findings will be explored in greater detail in the following chapters. Previous studies have found that children with ASD use fewer references to characters internal states, including their emotions, compared to typically developing children when telling a story (Losh and Capps, 2003; Siller *et al.*, 2014). Theory of mind involves the ability to recognise and understand one's own mental state as well as attribute these to others. There is a tendency for children with ASD to perform worse than typically developing children during tasks measuring theory of mind abilities (Baron-Cohen *et al.*, 1985; Happé, 1995; Losh and Capps, 2003; Tager-Flusberg, 2011). Thus, it is widely accepted that theory of mind is an impairment in ASD. Taking this into consideration, it can be predicted that individuals with ASD and ASD-LI will produce fewer references to frames of mind and emotive terms during the storytelling task compared to the DLD and TD groups. To date, the number of studies investigating the use of internal state language with individuals diagnosed with a language impairment is extremely limited in scope. Prior studies have found that children with SLI reference cognitive states as frequently as their typically developing peers when telling a story (Norbury and Bishop, 2003; Reilly *et al.*, 2004). Manolitsi and Botting (2011) reported that Greek children with SLI were more proficient in being able to reference characters goals and their actions compared to Greek children with ASD as well as produce the content of a story better. Considering that theory of mind is an impairment in ASD, it can be hypothesised that the children and adolescents with ASD and ASD-LI will produce fewer cognitive interjections than the DLD and TD groups during the storytelling task.

Emotive interjections convey the emotions and sensations that a speaker experiences at a given time. Emotions are a mental state therefore the ability to comprehend and recognise that another person can have a different emotional state to oneself is a fundamental part of theory of mind. Previous studies have found that children with ASD do not perform as well as their typically developing peers during emotion recognition tasks (Losh and Capps, 2003; Loukusa *et al.*, 2014; Taylor *et al.*, 2015). Some children with ASD, however, are as capable as typically developing individuals at recognising basic emotions (Castelli, 2005). Children with ASD have also been found to produce significantly fewer references to characters emotional states compared to typically developing children when telling a story (Losh and Capps, 2003; Siller *et al.*, 2014). In the present study, a narrative task was included to see whether speakers were able to correctly identify characters emotional states and express this through the use of interjections.

Wordless picture books have been used in previous studies to measure a person's linguistic abilities; as they do not contain any written text, they allow for the elicitation of language. The narrator has to form an interpretation about what is happening in the story based upon the illustrations depicted and the context. The narrator must also be able to decode characters facial expressions to allow for the attribution of characters emotional states. Thus, a narrative task was used in the current study with the aim of eliciting emotive interjections. The recognition and expression of emotions, however, are often treated as separate entities and they are rarely studied in conjunction with one-another. The number of studies investigating emotion recognition abilities using individuals with a language impairment is limited; thus, further research in this field is warranted. Previous studies have found that children with SLI did not differ from typically developing children when they were assessed on their emotion recognition abilities (Ford and Milosky, 2003; Loukusa *et al.*, 2014). Considering that the number of studies investigating emotional expression is extremely limited in scope, the findings from previous emotion recognition studies have been taken into account when formulating hypotheses about interjectional usage in the current study. With this in mind, it can be predicted that the children and adolescents with ASD and ASD-LI will produce fewer emotive interjections than the DLD and TD groups during both the storytelling task and play session.

Phatic interjections play an important role during social interactions as they can be used to maintain social and communicative contact between a speaker and listener; some examples include the discourse markers *uh-huh* or *mm* and they are often used by a listener to indicate that they are paying attention to a speaker's utterance during spoken discourse. Persistent deficits in social communication forms part of the triad of impairments in the diagnostic criteria for Autism Spectrum Disorder alongside social interaction and restricted, repetitive patterns of behaviour (American Psychiatric Association, 2013). Individuals with ASD tend to show less interest in engaging with others and initiating interactions, and they may have difficulties with turn-taking during a conversation. Gorman *et al.* (2016) found that children with ASD used the filler *uh-um* considerably less than the children with SLI and the typically developing children, who did not differ from one-another. *Uh-um* is often used to indicate agreement therefore it functions as a backchannelling device. Gorman *et al.*'s (2016) findings were based on transcripts of recorded sessions using the Autism Diagnostic Observation Schedule (ADOS, Lord *et al.*, 2000) which is a semi-structured, standardised assessment of social interaction, communication, and play. The sessions were composed of four different activities including make believe and joint interactive play, describing a picture, telling a story from a book, and conversation. Similarly, the methodological procedures in the current study were composed of participants generating a story using a wordless picture book and joint interactive play. Gorman *et al.* (2016) found that the children with ASD produced *um* significantly less than the children with SLI and the typically developing children, who did not differ from one-another. A study conducted by Irvine *et al.* (2016) reported similar results. *Um* is often used to indicate hesitation, however it can also be uttered by a speaker to signify agreement (Oxford English Dictionary, 1989). An association was detected between the severity of ASD and the use of the filler *um* therefore it can be suggested that *um* is characteristic of the social deficits in ASD as the filler serves a communicative function (Irvine *et al.* 2016). Considering that phatic interjections can be used to maintain social and communicative contact, which is an impairment in

ASD, it can be hypothesised that individuals with ASD and ASD-LI will produce fewer phatic interjections during the play session in comparison to the DLD and TD groups.

Volitive interjections are used to convey a person wanting something in the semantic meaning of their utterance. By expressing a person's wants, volitive interjections simultaneously express an internal mental state hereby exemplifying the close relation between cognitive and volitive interjections. Stange (2016) also asserts that volitive interjections can have an underlying emotive element; for example, a person may utter *ssh* if they become annoyed by the level of noise in the surrounding environment.

The study of interjections has been neglected by linguists to date. Previous studies have regarded interjections as not being an integral part of language on the basis that interjections are not standardised words as they do not conform to the conventionalised orthography and phonological rules of a language (Goffman, 1978). Consequently, there is the possibility that interjections have been omitted from transcripts of spoken discourse. There is also the possibility that interjections have been omitted from transcripts of narrative tasks as researchers tend to focus on the linguistic elements. This is noteworthy considering that characters internal mental states, including their emotions, can be expressed through the use of interjections. Thus far, no previous studies have included individuals with a neurodevelopmental disorder in their investigation into interjectional usage. This preliminary study is the first to do so, offering an insight into the different uses of emotive, cognitive, phatic, and volitive interjections by children and adolescents with ASD, ASD-LI, DLD, and a typically developing cohort.

6.8 Research Aims

As previously stated in the introduction to this book, the present research has two aims. The first aim of this study is to identify similarities and differences in the linguistic abilities of children and adolescents with Autism Spectrum Disorder (ASD), Autism Spectrum Disorder with an accompanying language impairment (ASD-LI), Developmental Language Disorder (DLD), and a typically developing (TD) cohort. The second aim is in fact the focal point of this study, and this involves investigating interjectional usage by children and adolescents with ASD, ASD-LI, DLD, and a TD cohort.

6.9　Hypotheses and Predictions

1. The TD and ASD groups will outperform the ASD-LI and the DLD groups on a number of linguistic measures, including performance on the BPVS-3 and CELF-5 assessments. Language difficulties as a result of comprehension and/or production deficits form the diagnostic criteria for DLD, and a language impairment co-occurs with ASD in the ASD-LI group. It is plausible to suggest that language difficulties will have a profound impact on a person's performance during the BPVS-3 and CELF-5 assessments in the current study.

2. Individuals with ASD and ASD-LI will produce fewer references to frames of mind and emotive terms during the storytelling task compared to the DLD and TD groups.

3. Individuals with ASD and ASD-LI will produce fewer cognitive interjections than the DLD and TD groups during the storytelling task.

4. Individuals with ASD and ASD-LI will produce fewer emotive interjections than the DLD and TD groups during both the storytelling task and play session.

5. Individuals with ASD and ASD-LI will produce fewer phatic interjections during the play session in comparison to the DLD and TD groups.

Chapter 7. Methodology

7.1 Participants

A total of 42 children and adolescents were initially recruited to take part in this study. However, three children with ASD-LI were excluded from taking part as they produced eight or more errors during the first set in the British Picture Vocabulary Scale – Third Edition (Dunn *et al.*, 2009). Thus, the ceiling set was established. Given that the first set is administered to children from the age of two years, it was concluded that the three children with ASD-LI would not be able to meet the demands of the tasks. This conclusion was also based upon observations made over the course of several months in regard to their receptive and expressive language abilities. Two typically developing children were unable to partake in the study as they moved schools before clinical assessments were due to commence. One typically developing child was excluded from further study after obtaining a score of below 77 on the Core Language Score and the Receptive Language Index from the Clinical Evaluation of Language Fundamentals – Fifth Edition (CELF-5, Wiig *et al.*, 2017). This score is indicative of an undiagnosed language impairment. Further clinical assessments, however, would need to be conducted to validate this finding. Thus, 36 children and adolescents participated in this study.

Firstly, participants were divided into four groups: Autism Spectrum Disorder (ASD), Autism Spectrum Disorder with an accompanying language impairment (ASD-LI), Developmental Language Disorder (DLD), and typical development. Clinical diagnoses were used to categorise the ASD, ASD-LI, and DLD groups accordingly. All children and adolescents identified as having ASD and ASD-LI had received a prior diagnosis based on criteria in the current DSM (American Psychiatric Association, 2013). This was confirmed by a speech and language therapist. All children and adolescents identified as having Developmental Language Disorder had received a diagnosis from the Special Educational Needs Teaching and Support Service (SENTASS) Specific Language Impairment Team, following a referral from specialist teachers and/or the NHS Speech and Language therapy service. This was confirmed by a speech and language therapist.

The CELF-5 (Wiig *et al.*, 2017) was administered to all participants. Language disorder was identified if an individual scored 77 or below (-1.5 *SD* below the mean) on their receptive, expressive, or core language index score. As expected, all participants with ASD-LI and DLD were confirmed as being linguistically impaired after scoring below 77 on the CELF-5 (Wiig *et al.*, 2017). Eligibility criteria required individuals to have English as their native language as well as having no history of a hearing impairment. Participants ranged in age from 7 years 4 months to 15 years 3 months old.

7.1.1 Participants with Autism Spectrum Disorder

The group of individuals with Autism Spectrum Disorder were formed of one child and four adolescents (ASD, N=5, M=12.18, SD=2.43). One child with ASD was recruited through an Additionally Resourced Centre for primary school aged children with communication difficulties. Four adolescents with ASD were recruited from a mainstream secondary school.

7.1.2 Participants with Autism Spectrum Disorder and a Language Impairment

Three children with Autism Spectrum Disorder and an accompanying language impairment (ASD-LI) were recruited through a specialist provision for primary school aged children with autism. Four children with ASD-LI were recruited through an Additionally Resourced Centre (ARC) for primary school aged children with a diagnosis of ASD. Four adolescents with ASD-LI were recruited from a mainstream secondary school. Thus, 8 children and 4 adolescents with Autism Spectrum Disorder and an accompanying language impairment comprised the final sample (ASD-LI, N=12, M=10.92, SD=2.48).

7.1.3 Participants with Developmental Language Disorder

Eleven participants formed the Developmental Language Disorder group, comprised of 9 children and 2 adolescents (DLD, N=11, M=10.05, SD=2.2). All nine children with DLD were recruited through a Speech and Language ARC for primary school aged children with a communication disorder. Two adolescents with DLD were recruited through a mainstream secondary school.

7.1.4 Typically Developing participants

Eight typically developing children participated in this study and they were recruited from a mainstream primary school (TD, N=8, M=9.56, SD=1.62). Eligibility criteria for this group consisted of having no history of language impairment, confirmed through parental verification and outcomes from conducting the CELF-5 (Wiig *et al.*, 2017) assessments with them. No typically developing adolescents participated in this study.

To summarise, the groups consisted of the following: Autism Spectrum Disorder (ASD, *N*=5, M=12.18, SD=2.43), Autism Spectrum Disorder with an accompanying language impairment (ASD-LI, *N*=12, M=10.92, SD=2.48), Developmental Language Disorder (DLD, *N*=11, M=10.05, SD=2.2), and typical development (TD, *N*=8, M=9.56, SD=1.62). The participants in this study were recruited from a number of different schools in the North East of England. Parental consent was obtained for all participants recruited through schools. Parents and children were provided with copies of an information sheet detailing what the study involved (see Appendix). It was made clear to each child that they did not have to take part and they could withdraw at any time if they wished. Those children whose parents deemed them able to give their own assent also gave written permission prior to commencing. The procedures of this study were approved by Newcastle University's Faculty of Medical Sciences Research Ethics Committee.

Groups	Mean age in years (SD)	Minimum age in years	Maximum age in years	*n* (% male)
Autism Spectrum Disorder (*n*=5)	12.18 (2.43)	8.58	14.39	4 (80%)
Autism Spectrum Disorder with a language impairment (*n*=12)	10.92 (2.48)	8.34	15.28	9 (75%)
Developmental Language Disorder (*n*=11)	10.05 (2.2)	7.73	14.65	6 (54.55%)
Typically Developing (*n*=8)	9.56 (1.62)	7.78	11.35	0 (0 %)

Table 2. Mean scores (SD) for chronological age

SD = Standard Deviation

Table 2 presents the mean ages and standard deviations for the four different groups: Autism Spectrum Disorder, Autism Spectrum Disorder with a language impairment, Developmental Language Disorder, and a typically developing cohort. Initially, the aim was to match participants according to age although difficulties arose during the recruitment process.

7.2   Materials, Design, and Procedures

7.2.1   British Picture Vocabulary Scale – Third Edition

Each person completed a one-to-one assessment using the British Picture Vocabulary Scale – Third Edition (BPVS-3, Dunn *et al.*, 2009), a standardised assessment used to measure receptive vocabulary. The BPVS-3 (Dunn *et al.*, 2009) is suitable for individuals from the age of 3 to 16 years 11 months. All participants were within this age range. As no written or verbal responses are required during the BPVS-3 (Dunn *et al.*, 2009) assessment, it can be administered to individuals with ASD and other communication difficulties as responses can be provided using gestures, including pointing to their chosen answer. The assessment is divided into fourteen sets according to chronological age, and administrators must use the appropriate set to determine the starting point. Firstly, the participant is presented with four images on each page. Upon hearing the administrator utter the test word, the participant must select one image corresponding to the word through providing a verbal response or gesturing towards their chosen answer. Each set contains twelve words, and the administrator must calculate the number of errors made by a participant in a set. The ceiling set is established when a participant makes eight or more errors per set, in which the administrator must discontinue testing. If the ceiling set is established during the first set, the administrator must use the preceding set and work backwards until the basal set is established. If a participant makes more than one error during the first set, but the ceiling has not yet been established, then the administrator must work backwards to establish the basal set before they can proceed to continue testing forward to establish the ceiling set. The basal set is established when a participant makes no more than one error per set. The BPVS-3 (Dunn *et al.*, 2009) was administered in one sitting with each participant.

7.2.2 *Clinical Evaluation of Language Fundamentals – Fifth Edition*

The Clinical Evaluation of Language Fundamentals – Fifth UK Edition (CELF-5, Wiig *et al.*, 2017) is a standardised assessment used to identify, diagnose, and provide an evaluation of a person's overall language abilities. The CELF-5 (Wiig *et al.*, 2017) provides an insight into a person's receptive and expressive language skills, core language abilities, and language use in relation to content. The distinction between them is as follows: receptive language assesses comprehension and listening, expressive scores measure oral language expression, core language scores measure a person's overall language ability, and language content is a measurement of a person's vocabulary and world knowledge. Thus, the CELF-5 (Wiig *et al.*, 2017) is used by speech and language therapists and professionals to identify language and communication disorders. The CELF-5 (Wiig *et al.*, 2017) contains a range of tests that can be individually administered, and it is suitable for individuals aged between 5 to 21 years 11 months. The full range of tests was administered to each participant with the exemption of the pragmatics profile, a new addition to the CELF-5 (Wiig *et al.*, 2017). The pragmatics profile was not administered as an insight into a person's overall language abilities could be obtained from the range of tests administered. The number of sessions and duration required to complete the CELF-5 (Wiig *et al.*, 2017) varied among participants. This is due to several factors such as attention and motivation to complete the tests. Taking this into consideration, administration of the tests over several sessions ensured that the assessments provided an accurate representation of a person's language abilities. Furthermore, time constraints to complete the assessments were imposed on by schools as a set duration of time was allocated in which participants could work with the researcher.

7.2.3 *Procedures*

The British Picture Vocabulary Scale – Third Edition (BPVS-3, Dunn *et al.*, 2009) and the Clinical Evaluation of Language Fundamentals – Fifth Edition (CELF-5, Wiig *et al.*, 2017) were conducted with all participants on a one-to-one basis, albeit in the presence of a speech and language therapist and/or class teacher. All participants had not undertaken the BPVS-3 (Dunn *et al.*, 2009) or the CELF-5 (Wiig *et al.*, 2017) assessments within the last six months, and this was confirmed by a speech and language therapist. The results provided an up-to-date score for all participants at the time of study. The assessments were conducted in a quiet room, except for two schools whereby they did not have the available facilities to accommodate for this. Under these circumstances, the assessments were conducted in a quieter section of the classroom where possible.

7.2.4 Pilot Study

Prior to commencing the narrative task, a pilot study was conducted with three typically developing children to ensure the demands of the task were met. All three children were aged 8 years old and they had no reported history of speech or language impairments. This was confirmed through parental and teacher verification. Written consent was obtained from both parents and children, and participants provided verbal assent prior to commencing the task. Participants were informed that they did not have to take part in the pilot study, and they could withdraw at any point if they wished to do so. The pilot study was not audio recorded, and the participants were excluded from taking part in the remainder of the study. Verbal instructions were provided to each participant before commencing the pilot study and their comprehension of the task was acknowledged. The first two pages of the book was narrated to them, and participants were then instructed to continue telling the rest of the story. This format was formerly used in Siller *et al.*'s (2014) study. Once the participants began their narrative, they were not interrupted unless clarification of a statement was required or to provide encouragement for the elaboration of ideas deemed essential for the continuation of their narrative.

7.2.5 Narrative Task

This preliminary study is the first to use a narrative task to elicit interjections. Narratives can provide an insight into a person's cognitive, linguistic, and social abilities. With regard to cognition, interjections can be used to express the attitude or mental state of a speaker (Fraser, 1990; Ameka, 1992; Wierzbicka, 1992; Metcalfe *et al.*, 2009; Wharton, 2009; Stange, 2016; Downing and Martínez Caro, 2019). Thus, a narrative task was included to see whether speakers are able to express characters internal mental states, including their emotions, through the use of interjections. The ability to attribute mental states to other people is an integral feature of storytelling as it can be used to explain character's behaviour and their actions as a result of their internal states (Tager-Flusberg and Sullivan, 1995; Capps *et al.*, 2000; Norbury and Bishop, 2003; Norbury *et al.*, 2014). This is a component of theory of mind. Also, story generation tasks are a particularly useful method to elicit language which can be examined for references to frames of mind.

Narratives were elicited using the picture book *Hug* (Alborough, 2000). The book contains 30 pages of illustrations and there are only three words included in the story: *hug, Bobo*, and *mummy*. To rule out the possibility that participants could not read the word *hug*, they were instructed to read the title of the book before commencing the task. The book depicts a range of different emotions thereby providing an opportunity for the narrator to describe the protagonists internal cognitive and emotional states. The plotline consists of a baby chimpanzee, named Bobo, embarking on a quest to find his mother after becoming lost wandering through a jungle. Bobo passes several different species of animals embracing one-another, and as he does so he utters the word *hug*. Witnessing other animals hug one-another soon causes Bobo to become distressed, as illustrated in the left-hand image in Figure 6. A mother elephant helps Bobo find his own mother, and they are soon reunited as she emerges after hearing Bobo's wails. Expressing his gratitude for helping him, Bobo hugs the mother elephant. This is illustrated in the right-hand image in Figure 6. All the animals rejoice and embrace one-another, shouting the word *hug*. According to the author, the use of the word *hug* at this point in the story symbolises unity and the animals' need for one-another (Alborough, no date). The story ends with Bobo and his mother leaving hand-in-hand with one another. Participants were provided with verbal instructions before commencing the narrative task and their comprehension was acknowledged. The first two pages of the book was narrated to them, and participants were then instructed to continue telling the rest of the story. Once the participants began their narrative, they were not interrupted unless clarification of a statement was required or to provide encouragement for the elaboration of ideas deemed essential for the continuation of their narrative. Narratives were audio recorded using an Olympus WS-852 digital stereo voice recorder and then transcribed by the researcher according to the Codes for Human Analysis of Transcripts (CHAT, McWhinney, 2000).

As there is an extremely limited amount of text contained within the book, the reader must be able to form an inference about the different underlying meanings of the word *hug* by considering the different contextual circumstances. At the beginning of the story, it can be interpreted that Bobo uttered *hug* to state the physical actions of the other animals embracing one-another (Alborough, no date). The same word conveys different communicative intentions as the story develops. For example, it can be proposed that Bobo utters the word *hug* to express his desire for a hug whereas *hug* is later uttered to communicate that he wants his mother (Alborough, no date). Context plays an important part in allowing a reader to formulate inferences about characters' communicative intentions.

Figure 6. Illustrations from the book *Hug* (Alborough, 2000)

Analysis of Narrative Ability

Length

Story length was calculated by measuring the total number of utterances produced by each participant and calculating the mean length of each utterance. Story length was also measured by calculating the total number of propositions produced and the total number of words. A proposition is defined as a complete phrase consisting of a verb and its arguments (Botting, 2002). Thus, a single proposition must contain a minimum of one verb and one noun (Botting, 2002). With regard to semantics, one proposition typically equates to a single event (Capps *et al.*, 2000, p. 196). For example, the utterance, "Bobo wanted a hug" was coded as one proposition whereas "Bobo cried on a rock and all the animals gathered around him" counted as two propositions.

Morphological errors

Morphemes are defined as the smallest unit of language. Morphological errors were analysed according to type and frequency. These included errors of omission such as auxiliaries (e.g., "*Bobo 0 walking along the path*") and determiners (e.g., "*0 monkey is sad*"). Errors of commission were also analysed including over-regularisations (e.g., "*Bobo sitted on a rock*"), agreement errors (e.g., "Bobo *sit* on a rock and cried"), and pronoun errors (e.g., "*him* cried when he lost *him* mummy").

Narrative evaluation

Evaluative devices were measured as they provide an insight into a narrators' perspective and their understanding of a story, extending beyond describing events (Bamberg and Damrad-Frye, 1991). Evaluative devices were analysed based on the five different categories outlined in Bamberg and Damrad-Frye's (1991) study: these include references to frames of mind, the use of character speech, hedges, negative propositions, and causal statements.

1. Frames of mind – The number of references to characters frames of mind were calculated. This includes terms used to refer to affective and emotional states (e.g., *happy, sad*), behavioural terms (e.g., *cry*), and terms relating to cognition (e.g., *thinking, know, decide, wonder*).
2. Character Speech – The use of character speech demonstrates a narrator's ability to adopt the perspective of a character (e.g., "Bobo said, '*Please will you help me find my mummy?*"). The latter is an example of direct speech. Indirect speech was also included in this category (e.g., "Bobo said *thank you* to the mother elephant for helping him try to find his mother").
3. Hedges – The use of hedges suggests that the truth value of a proposition is not definitive therefore alternative interpretations of an event are possible (e.g., "Bobo *might* want a hug"). Hedges are indicative of a narrators' uncertainty about an episode within a story.
4. Negatives – Negative propositions provide an insight into a narrator's perspective and their understanding of a story as they indicate events or behaviours which are contradictory to underlying expectations (e.g., "Bobo *didn't* know where his mummy was").
5. Causal statements – Causal statements involve the narrator forming an inference about the causes or motivations which underlie the behaviour of characters or certain events in a story (e.g., "Bobo was sad *because* he couldn't find his mummy").

Analysis of Narrative Performance

Narrative performance was also measured in accordance with the categories outlined in Wetherell *et al.*'s (2007) study. This includes the following three categories:

1. Total number of prompts – the quantity of utterances produced by the researcher was calculated if it was deemed necessary for participants continuation of a narrative (e.g., "*Can you tell me what is happening in the story?*").
2. Total number of fillers – the quantity of fillers produced by each participant was calculated as a measurement of narrative disfluency (e.g., *er, um, mm*).
3. Total number of corrections – the quantity of retracing and false starts, with and without corrections, was calculated as a measure of narrative disfluency.

Non-narrator speech

The number of propositions classed as non-narrator speech was calculated as this is a measure of narrative disfluency. This involved stepping out of the narrator role to ask questions or provide a commentary.

Types of Interjections

The number of interjections produced was calculated, based on the following categories: cognitive, emotive, phatic, and volitive. These results were then sub-divided to distinguish between the use of interjections produced during character speech and non-character speech. An example of narrator speech includes '*He thought **wow** to himself. I wish I could do that*'. By contrast, '***Ah** this is quite sad*' is an example of non-narrator speech providing a commentary on the story.

7.2.6 Play Method

Play sessions have been fruitful in eliciting interjections in previous studies. Stange (2016) used transcripts of recorded children's play sessions in her investigation into emotive interjections in British English. Additionally, Gorman *et al.* (2016) used transcripts of play sessions in his analyses of fillers produced by children diagnosed with ASD, SLI, and typical development. These studies, combined with the observations I made while working in a variety of different educational settings, were influential in the process of deciding which methodological procedures should be used in the current study. For example, I observed one pupil with ASD, Jack, build a Lego model independently. Jack dropped a piece of Lego which fell onto the floor and, as this happened, he uttered the interjection *oops* instinctively. On a separate occasion, I played a board game with the aforementioned pupil with ASD. The premise of the game was to build an ice-cream sundae and the first person do so is the winner. Players take it in turns to spin a wheel, and each section is partitioned into different flavours. According to the rules of the game, each flavour can only appear once in the ice-cream sundae. During the game, Jack spun the wheel and the arrow landed on the strawberry flavour. As Jack had previously landed on this flavour, he had to miss a turn. Upon realising this, Jack uttered the interjection '*Oh no!*' After managing to build the ice-cream sundae first, Jack congratulated me by uttering '*Well done!*' While working in a mainstream primary school, I observed a group of typically developing pupils utter the interjection *yay* in unison when the teacher told the class they could play games for the remainder of the lesson as it was the last day of term.

Spontaneous speech was elicited through playing the board game snakes and ladders with participants one-to-one in the present study. Thirty minutes of audio recordings were elicited through playing one or more games with each participant. Two children with ASD-LI were not willing to continue playing after losing a game, therefore several play sessions were required to obtain the desired length of audio recordings. Participants played snakes and ladders in a quiet room, except for two schools whereby they did not have the resources available to accommodate for this. Under these circumstances, the game was conducted in a quieter section of the classroom.

Prior to commencing the game, participants were provided with instructions on how to play and their comprehension was acknowledged. Players decided amongst themselves who should start. According to the rules of the game, players start from the first square and take it in turns to roll a die. Based upon the number rolled, players move their counter accordingly. Players climb up a ladder if they land on a square containing the base of a ladder, and they slide down to the bottom of a snake if they land on a square containing the head of a snake. The first person to reach the highest number, 100, on the board wins. The same Olympus WS-852 digital stereo voice recorder was used to record audio during the board game task. The audio recordings were then transcribed by the researcher according to the CHAT manual (McWhinney, 2000). The number of interjections produced was calculated, based on the following categories: cognitive, emotive, phatic, and volitive. The number of fillers produced was also calculated as they provide an insight into a speaker's cognitive state. The frequency of interjections was also calculated.

7.3 Data Analysis

Data analysis was performed using IBM SPSS Statistics (Version 26). Descriptive statistics were calculated for the ASD, ASD-LI, DLD, and TD samples. As the group sizes were unequal, the non-parametric Kruskal-Wallis one-way analysis of variance (ANOVA) test was used to detect for significances in the distribution of the data. This test determines whether there are significant differences in the distribution of the data at the $p = 0.05$ level. Where significant differences were detected, pairwise comparisons of group categories were conducted using the Bonferroni correction for multiple tests. This identifies where there are group differences, and significance levels were set at the $p = 0.05$ level. The non-parametric Spearman's Rho test was used to measure the strength of association between two values. The Spearman correlation coefficient indicates a positive association of ranks if the value is +1, whereas a value of 0 indicates no association and a value of -1 indicates a negative association of ranks.

Chapter 8. Results

Descriptive statistics for group performance on the BPVS-3 (Dunn *et al.*, 2009) and CELF-5 (Wiig *et al.*, 2017) assessments are presented in Table 3. Standardised scores could not be computed for all participants using the BPVS-3 (Dunn *et al.*, 2009). This was due to some participants obtaining extremely low scores, therefore mean raw scores were calculated instead for the BPVS-3 (Dunn *et al.*, 2009). Standardised scores, however, were used for all language measures assessed through the CELF-5 (Wiig *et al.*, 2017).

Groups	BPVS-3 Raw Score	CELF-5 Receptive Language Score	CELF-5 Expressive Language Score	CELF-5 Core Language Score	CELF-5 Language Content Score
Autism Spectrum Disorder (*n*=5)	146.2 (6.26)	100.6 (7.33)	93.8 (9.83)	93 (12.33)	107 (13.34)
Autism Spectrum Disorder with a language impairment (*n*=12)	101.83 (29.58)	70.67 (12.70)	66.08 (9.95)	66.91 (11.29)	69.92 (10.79)
Developmental Language Disorder (*n*=11)	81.27 (20.16)	65.9 (9.45)	57.27 (5.85)	57.9 (8.25)	65.45 (9.00)
Typically Developing (*n*=8)	121.5 (19.41)	101.88 (7.59)	95.88 (14.28)	97.88 (12.11)	105.25 (6.04)

Table 3.   Mean scores (SD) on clinical assessments

SD = Standard Deviation

8.1 British Picture Vocabulary Scale – Third Edition

The BPVS-3 (Dunn et al., 2009) was used to measure participants receptive vocabulary abilities. To detect whether there were notable differences between groups in regard to BPVS-3 (Dunn et al., 2009) raw scores, the Kruskal-Wallis one-way ANOVA was conducted. This confirmed that the distribution of BPVS-3 raw scores were significantly different between the groups ($H(3) = 19.173$, $p = <0.001$). To distinguish where groups significantly differed from one-another, the Bonferroni correction for multiple tests was used. This revealed that the raw scores for the ASD group were significantly higher than the ASD-LI group ($p = 0.039$) and the DLD group ($p = <0.001$). Interestingly, the ASD and TD groups did not differ from one another significantly ($p = 0.648$). There were no significant differences found between the ASD-LI group and the DLD group ($p = 0.379$), and the TD group ($p = 1.000$). The BPVS-3 raw scores for the DLD group were significantly lower than the ASD and TD groups ($p = 0.029$), although they did not differ from the ASD-LI cohort. To clarify, the BPVS-3 raw scores for the TD group were significantly higher than the ASD-LI and DLD groups. However, no significant differences were detected between the TD and the ASD group. The ASD-LI and DLD groups did not differ from one-another.

To assess whether age had a confounding effect upon BPVS-3 raw scores, adjustment for age was carried out using multiple regression modelling. After adjustment, the expected value for the BPVS-3 raw score for the TD group was higher than the DLD group ($\beta = 43.632$) and the difference between the groups was significant ($p = <0.001$). Similarly, the expected value for the BPVS-3 raw score for the ASD group was higher than the DLD group ($\beta = 50.402$) and the groups were significantly different ($p = <0.001$). Although the expected value for the ASD-LI group was higher than the DLD group ($\beta = 14.613$), this difference just failed to reach significance levels ($p = 0.052$). Overall, these results indicate that there are remarkable similarities between the ASD-LI and DLD groups in regard to receptive vocabulary abilities. Also, these results confirm that receptive language was not impaired in the ASD group and they performed as well as the typically developing children. This is illustrated in Table 3.

8.2 Clinical Evaluation of Language Fundamentals – Fifth Edition

Receptive Language Index scores

To assess whether groups differed in regard to CELF-5 Receptive Language Index (RLI) standardised scores, the Kruskal-Wallis one-way ANOVA was used. This confirmed there were significant differences in the distribution of RLI scores between groups ($H(3) = 24.130$, $p = <0.001$). Pairwise comparisons using the Bonferroni correction for multiple tests revealed that the RLI scores for the ASD group were significantly higher than the ASD-LI ($p = 0.027$) and DLD groups ($p = 0.005$). Interestingly, no differences were detected between the ASD and TD groups ($p = 1.000$). The RLI scores for the ASD-LI group were significantly lower than the ASD group, as previously stated, and the TD group ($p = 0.003$). However, the ASD-LI and DLD group did not differ from one-another ($p = 1.000$). RLI scores for the DLD group were significantly lower than the ASD group and the TD group ($p = <0.001$). This result is not surprising considering that a language disorder is diagnosed on the premise of comprehension and/or production deficits. It is worth highlighting that no significant differences were detected between the DLD and the ASD-LI groups, thereby demonstrating their interrelation. To clarify, the CELF-5 Receptive Language Index standardised scores for the TD group were significantly higher than the ASD-LI and the DLD groups. However, no significant differences were detected between the TD and the ASD groups. The ASD-LI and DLD groups did not differ from one-another.

Expressive Language Index scores

The Kruskal-Wallis one-way ANOVA was used to determine whether there were differences in the CELF-5 Expressive Language Index (ELI) standardised scores and group categories. This statistical test confirmed significant differences ($H(3) = 26.615$, $p = <0.001$). Pairwise comparisons using the Bonferroni correction for multiple tests revealed that the ELI scores for the ASD group were significantly higher than the ASD-LI ($p = 0.05$) and the DLD groups ($p = 0.001$). However, the ASD and TD groups did not differ from one-another ($p = 1.000$). The ELI scores for the ASD-LI group were significantly lower than the ASD group, as previously stated, and the TD group ($p = 0.012$). The ASD-LI and DLD groups did not differ from one-another ($p = 0.761$). Meanwhile, the ELI scores for the DLD group were significantly lower than the ASD group and the TD group ($p = <0.001$). To clarify, the CELF-5 Expressive Language Index standardised scores for the TD group were significantly higher than the ASD-

LI and the DLD groups. However, no significant differences were detected between the TD and ASD groups. The ASD-LI and DLD groups did not differ from one-another.

Core Language scores

There were significant differences detected between CELF-5 Core Language standardised scores and group categories, confirmed using the Kruskal-Wallis one-way ANOVA ($H(3) = 25.489$, $p = <0.001$). Pairwise comparisons using the Bonferroni correction for multiple tests revealed that the ASD group did not differ from the ASD-LI ($p = 0.086$) and the TD groups ($p = 1.000$) in regard to Core Language scores. However, the Core Language scores for the ASD group were significantly higher compared to the DLD group ($p = 0.003$). Interestingly, the ASD-LI group did not differ from the ASD and the DLD groups ($p = 1.000$). The Core Language Scores for the ASD-LI group, however, were significantly lower than the TD group ($p = 0.006$). Meanwhile, the Core Language scores for the DLD group were significantly lower than the ASD group ($p = 0.003$) and the TD group ($p = <0.001$). To clarify, the ASD group did not differ from the ASD-LI and the TD groups in regard to CELF-5 Core Language standardised scores. Both the ASD and the TD groups performed significantly better than the DLD group when core language scores were assessed. The TD group performed significantly better than the ASD-LI group when they were assessed on their core language abilities, although the ASD-LI and the DLD groups did not differ from one-another.

Language Content Index scores

To assess whether groups differed in regard to CELF-5 Language Content Index (LCI) standardised scores, the Kruskal-Wallis one-way ANOVA was used. This confirmed that there were significant differences in the distribution of LCI scores among groups ($H(3) = 24.939$, $p = <0.001$). Pairwise comparisons using the Bonferroni correction for multiple tests revealed that the LCI scores for the ASD group were significantly higher than the ASD-LI ($p = 0.025$) and the DLD groups ($p = 0.004$). However, the ASD and the TD groups did not differ from one-another ($p = 1.000$). Additionally, the LCI scores for the ASD-LI group were significantly lower than the ASD group and the TD groups ($p = 0.003$). No significant differences were found between the ASD-LI and the DLD groups ($p = 1.000$). Meanwhile, the LCI scores for the DLD group were substantially lower than the ASD group, as previously stated, and the TD group ($p = <0.001$). To clarify, the Language Content Index standardised scores for the TD group were significantly higher than the ASD-LI and the DLD groups. No significant differences were detected between the TD and the ASD groups. The ASD-LI and DLD groups did not differ from one-another.

8.3 Language Abilities during the Narrative Task

Table 4 presents a breakdown of mean scores and standard deviation for a range of different linguistic measures produced during the narrative task. This is presented on the following page. To reiterate, the task involved generating a story using the picture book *Hug* by Jez Alborough.

	ASD (*n*=5)	ASD-LI (*n*=12)	DLD (*n*=11)	TD (*n*=8)
Total utterances	27.4 (10.24)	30.17 (10.90)	33.91 (7.93)	30.13 (8.29)
Total number of words	271.6 (111.64)	220.33 (104.40)	165.73 (90.23)	352.13 (161.67)
Mean length of utterance	10.12 (2.04)	7.38 (3.07)	4.91 (2.06)	12.76 (7.57)
Number of propositions	29.8 (14.02)	27.92 (13.30)	20.91 (10.08)	39.00 (12.33)
Auxiliary omissions	0.20 (0.45)	1.25 (1.91)	2.82 (3.40)	0.75 (0.71)
Determiner omissions	0.20 (0.45)	2.08 (3.98)	1.18 (1.54)	0.75 (0.89)
Over-regularisations	0.00 (0.00)	0.42 (0.69)	0.00 (0.00)	0.00 (0.00)
Agreement errors	0.00 (0.00)	1.92 (1.51)	6.36 (5.64)	2.63 (2.72)
Pronoun errors	0.00 (0.00)	0.17 (0.39)	1.45 (3.88)	0.13 (0.35)

Table 4. Mean scores (SD) of linguistic measures during the narrative task

SD = Standard Deviation

To compare the differences between groups on a range of linguistic measures, the Kruskal-Wallis one-way ANOVA was used. Surprisingly, the groups did not differ from one-another in regard to the total number of utterances produced during the narrative task ($H(3) = 1.977$, $p = 0.577$). Nevertheless, group differences were detected on a number of other linguistic measures which shall be addressed in this section. For example, pairwise comparisons using the Bonferroni correction for multiple tests revealed that the DLD cohort produced significantly fewer words compared to the TD group during the narrative task ($p = 0.022$). No other group differences were reported in regard to this measure. Additionally, the utterances produced by the DLD group were significantly shorter compared to those produced by the ASD ($p = 0.024$) and the TD group ($p = 0.006$). No significant differences were detected between the DLD and the ASD-LI groups when mean length of utterance was calculated ($p = 0.469$), nor were any other group differences found. Furthermore, significantly fewer propositions were produced by the DLD group in comparison to the TD group ($p = 0.029$). This failed to reach the significance level at $p = 0.05$ with the ASD and ASD-LI groups. It is worth noting that the ASD, ASD-LI, and TD groups did not differ from one-another in regard to the number of propositions produced during the storytelling task. Additionally, the DLD group produced significantly more auxiliary omissions ($p = 0.04$) and agreement errors ($p = 0.003$) during the narrative task compared to the ASD group. This failed to reach significance levels with the ASD-LI group and more surprisingly, the TD group. No significant differences between groups were detected in regard to the number of over-regularisations, omission of determiners, and pronoun errors used during the narrative task.

The Use of Evaluative Devices

Evaluative devices are an important component of storytelling as they provide an insight into the narrator's perspective and understanding of a story. Evaluative devices were composed of references to frames of mind, causal statements, character speech, hedges, and the use of negative propositions. The descriptive statistics for frames of mind references, produced during the narrative task, are presented in Table 5. This is one element of evaluative devices. References to frames of mind were further sub-divided into emotional, behavioural, and cognitive terms as illustrated in Table 5.

	ASD (*n*=5)	ASD-LI (*n*=12)	DLD (*n*=11)	TD (*n*=8)
Frames of mind	8.80 (4.21)	8.58 (5.00)	6.90 (5.15)	13.00 (6.44)
Number of emotion terms	3.00 (2.12)	3.17 (3.04)	4.18 (4.73)	6.13 (3.83)
Number of behavioural terms	4.00 (2.55)	3.50 (3.09)	1.73 (1.35)	4.38 (1.77)
Number of cognitive terms	1.80 (2.05)	1.92 (2.78)	1.00 (1.18)	2.50 (2.45)

Table 5. Mean scores (SD) on frames of mind references during storytelling

SD = Standard Deviation

Closer inspection of Table 5 shows that the TD children produced more references to frames of mind during the narrative task overall. Despite this, no significant differences were detected between groups in regard to the number of frames of mind references produced during the storytelling task ($H(3) = 5.576$, $p = 0.134$). This was confirmed using the Kruskal-Wallis one-way ANOVA. Furthermore, no significant group differences were found in regard to emotive terms ($H(3) = 4.354$, $p = 0.226$), behavioural references, ($H(3) = 7.714$, $p = 0.52$), and cognitive terms ($H(3) = 1.742$, $p = 0.628$) produced during the storytelling task.

The descriptive statistics for the remaining evaluative devices produced during the story-telling task are presented in Table 6, based on group categories.

	ASD (*n*=5)	ASD-LI (*n*=12)	DLD (*n*=11)	TD (*n*=8)
Causal statements	0.80 (0.84)	0.67 (0.89)	1.00 (1.10)	4.13 (5.25)
Character speech	9.60 (3.97)	7.08 (4.08)	3.36 (2.34)	10.50 (4.00)
Number of hedges	0.00 (0.00)	0.17 (0.39)	0.18 (0.60)	1.25 (2.38)
Negative propositions	2.20 (3.03)	1.17 (2.17)	1.18 (1.60)	1.75 (2.05)

Table 6.   Mean scores (SD) on evaluative devices used during storytelling

SD = Standard Deviation

Closer inspection of Table 6 shows that the TD children produced more causal statements, instances of character speech, and hedges. Despite this, group differences in regard to the number of causal statements produced during the narrative task failed to reach significance levels ($H(3) = 1.742$, $p = 0.628$). Similarly, no significant group differences were reported in regard to the number of hedges produced ($H(3) = 6.444$, $p = 0.092$) and the number of negative propositions used during the narrative task ($H(3) = 0.776$, $p = 0.855$). However, significant differences were detected between groups in the use of character speech ($H(3) = 14.415$, $p = 0.002$). These findings were confirmed using the Kruskal-Wallis one-way ANOVA. Pairwise comparisons using the Bonferroni correction method for multiple tests revealed that the DLD group used character speech significantly less than the TD group ($p = 0.003$). No significant differences were detected between the DLD and the ASD-LI cohorts in regard to this ($p = 0.190$). Although the DLD group produced fewer instances of character speech in comparison to the ASD group, this narrowly failed to reach significance levels ($p = 0.054$). No other group differences were detected. Finally, no significant differences were detected between groups in regard to the number of negative propositions used during the narrative task ($H(3) = 0.776$, $p = 0.855$).

Narrative Performance

Narrative performance was measured using a number of different features. Firstly, the number of prompts required, which were essential for the continuation of a narrative, were calculated. In addition, the number of fillers produced were calculated. Prompts and fillers provide an insight into a narrator's cognitive state. For example, frequent use of prompts and fillers can indicate that a speaker is having difficulty interpreting the illustrations depicted in a book and/or having difficulty constructing an utterance during a storytelling task. The number of corrections produced was also calculated as this is a measure of narrative disfluency. Additionally, the number of propositions produced during non-narrator speech was calculated as this consists of a person stepping outside of the narrator role. This often included asking questions (e.g., "*Is that an iguana?*") or making a commentary about the story. The number of interjections produced were also calculated, both within character and non-character speech. Table 7 shows the breakdown of mean scores and standard deviation between groups on a range of different measures of narrative performance.

	ASD (*n*=5)	ASD-LI (*n*=12)	DLD (*n*=11)	TD (*n*=8)
Prompts	0.00 (0.00)	0.83 (0.29)	1.64 (2.11)	0.00 (0.00)
Fillers	1.40 (0.89)	3.00 (8.06)	4.82 (4.21)	1.13 (1.64)
Corrections	6.80 (4.86)	7.41 (7.87)	3.55 (3.42)	5.63 (4.31)
Non-narrator speech	2.80 (3.42)	1.42 (2.87)	4.27 (3.85)	1.25 (1.58)
Number of interjections	1.20 (1.30)	0.67 (1.23)	1.73 (2.24)	0.25 (0.46)

Table 7. Mean scores (SD) on narrative performance

SD = Standard Deviation

Although the features are used sparingly, closer inspection of Table 7 reveals that the DLD group used more instances of prompts, fillers, non-narrator speech and interjections compared to the other three groups. The Kruskal-Wallis one-way ANOVA confirmed that the distribution of non-narrator speech between groups was not significant ($H(3) = 6.432, p = 0.092$), nor were the number of interjections produced during the narrative task ($H(3) = 3.805, p = 0.283$). There were no significant group differences in regard to the type of interjections used during the narrative task: this includes cognitive ($H(3) = 4.118, p = 0.249$), emotive ($H(3) = 1.654, p = 0.647$), phatic ($H(3) = <0.001, p = 1.000$), and volitive interjections ($H(3) = <0.001, p = 1.000$).

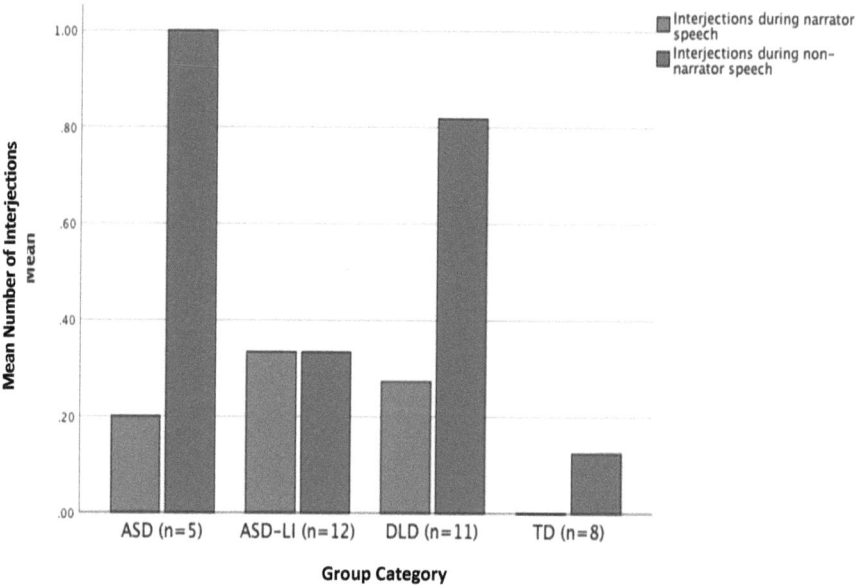

Figure 7. A bar chart representing the mean number of interjections produced during narrator and non-narrator speech, based on group categories.

Pairwise comparisons revealed that during the narrative task, the DLD group required significantly more prompts by the researcher compared to the ASD, ASD-LI, and TD groups ($p = <0.05$). No other group differences were detected. With regard to the number of fillers produced during the narrative task, no differences were reported between the DLD group and the ASD ($p = 1.000$) and TD groups ($p = 0.283$). Interestingly, the DLD group produced significantly more fillers than the ASD-LI group during the storytelling task ($p = 0.036$). No other group differences were reported.

	ASD (n=5)	ASD-LI (n=12)	DLD (n=11)	TD (n=8)
Cognitive	0.00 (0.00)	0.17 (0.39)	0.00 (0.00)	0.00 (0.00)
Emotive	0.20 (0.45)	0.17 (0.39)	0.27 (0.65)	0.00 (0.00)
Phatic	0.00 (0.00)	0.00 (0.00)	0.00 (0.00)	0.00 (0.00)
Volitive	0.00 (0.00)	0.08 (0.29)	0.00 (0.00)	0.00 (0.00)

Table 8. **Mean scores (SD) on the type of interjections produced during narrator speech in the storytelling task**

SD = Standard Deviation

Cognitive, emotive, phatic, and volitive interjections were used sparingly by all four groups during narrator speech in the storytelling task; this is illustrated in Table 8. Thus, no group differences were found in regard to the distribution of cognitive ($H(3) = 4.118, p = 0.249$), emotive ($H(3) = 1.654, p = 0.647$), phatic ($H(3) = <0.001, p = 1.000$), and volitive interjections ($H(3) = <0.001, p = 1.000$) embedded within narrator speech in the storytelling task. These findings were confirmed using the Kruskal-Wallis one-way ANOVA.

To detect whether there were any correlations between variables, the non-parametric Spearman's Rho test was used as group sizes were unequal. The result is significant at $p = 0.05$ level. The test detected an association between the use of cognitive interjections during narrator speech and CELF-5 Receptive Language Index scores for the ASD-LI group ($r = 0.586, p = 0.45$). Also, the number of utterances was associated with emotive interjections during narrator speech for the ASD-LI group ($r = 0.583, p = 0.047$). For the DLD group, emotive interjections were associated with CELF-5 Receptive Language Index ($r = 0.676, p = 0.022$) and CELF-5 Language Content scores ($r = 0.677, p = 0.022$). Additionally, emotive interjections were associated with emotion terms used during the narrative task for the DLD group ($r = 0.654, p = 0.029$), as well as character speech ($r = 0.659, p = 0.028$). No other correlations were detected.

	ASD (n=5)	ASD-LI (n=12)	DLD (n=11)	TD (n=8)
Cognitive	0.40 (0.55)	0.25 (0.62)	0.73 (1.27)	0.13 (0.35)
Emotive	0.40 (0.55)	0.00 (0.00)	0.09 (0.30)	0.00 (0.00)
Phatic	0.00 (0.00)	0.00 (0.00)	0.00 (0.00)	0.00 (0.00)
Volitive	0.20 (0.45)	0.09 (0.30)	0.00 (0.00)	0.00 (0.00)

Table 9. Mean scores (SD) on the type of interjections produced during non-narrator speech in the storytelling task

SD = Standard Deviation

Similarly, cognitive, emotive, phatic, and volitive interjections were used sparingly by all four groups during non-narrator speech in the storytelling task; this is illustrated in Table 9. No group differences were detected in regard to the distribution of cognitive (H(3) = 2.436, p = 0.487), phatic (H(3) = <0.001, p = 1.000), and volitive interjections (H(3) = 3.191, p = 0.363) produced during non-narrator speech in the storytelling task. However, group differences emerged in the use of emotive interjections during non-narrator speech in the storytelling task (H(3) = 8.157, p = 0.043). These findings were confirmed using the Kruskal-Wallis one-way ANOVA. Pairwise comparisons using the Bonferroni correction for multiple tests revealed that the ASD group produced significantly more emotive interjections than the ASD-LI group (p = 0.038) during non-narrator speech. No other group differences were detected. It is worth noting, however, that the ASD group produced more emotive interjections than the TD cohort although it failed to reach significance levels (p = 0.061).

8.3.1   The Relationship between Language Abilities and Narrative Measures

To detect whether there were any correlations between variables, the non-parametric Spearman's Rho test was used as group sizes were unequal. The result is significant at p = 0.05 level. The test detected that age was associated with BPVS-3 raw scores for the ASD, ASD-LI, DLD, and TD groups. Age, however, was not associated with any of the CELF-5 language measures for all four groups. The interrelation between language and emotion can be exemplified through the association found between BPVS-3 raw scores and references to frames of mind: this includes emotive terms (r = 0.338, p = 0.44), behavioural references, (r = 0.468, p = 0.004), and terms relating to cognition (r = 0.396, p = 0.017). Additionally, references to frames of mind during the storytelling task were significantly associated with all of the CELF-5 language measures (Receptive Language Index: $r = 0.401$, $p = 0.015$; Expressive Language Index: $r = 0.452$, $p = 0.006$; Core Language score: $r = 0.470$, $p = 0.004$; Language Content Index: $r = 0.483$, $p = 0.003$). Taken together, these findings indicate that language and emotion are interrelated.

There were notable discrepancies between the groups in regard to narrative measures. The following results should be interpreted with caution due to the small sample sizes. For the ASD group, references to frames of mind were associated with the number of words produced during the storytelling task ($r = 0.900$, $p = 0.037$). The number of propositions was associated with the use of emotion terms for the ASD group ($r = 0.895$, $p = 0.040$) and the ASD-LI group ($r = 0.615$, $p = 0.033$) in the narrative task. Interestingly, no associations were found between the number of propositions used and emotive terms for the DLD and the TD groups. For the ASD-LI group, the number of propositions produced during storytelling was associated with behavioural terms ($r = 0.707$, $p = 0.010$) and the use of character speech ($r = 0.713$, $p = 0.009$). This finding was not applicable to the ASD group. References to frames of mind were associated with a range of different language measures used during the narrative task for the ASD-LI group: this includes the number of words produced ($r = 0.811$, $p = 0.001$), mean length of utterance ($r = 0.857$, $p = <0.001$), propositions ($r = 0.816$, $p = 0.001$), and causal statements ($r = 0.730$, $p = 0.007$). Interestingly, the use of emotive terms was significantly associated with interjections produced during narrator speech for the ASD-LI group ($r = 0.604$, $p = 0.038$). This result exemplifies the significance of interjections in conveying emotional states. Moreover, references to frames of mind were associated with BPVS-3 raw scores ($r = 0.674$, $p = 0.16$), CELF-5 Core Language scores ($r = 0.654$, $p = 0.021$), and Language Content Index scores ($r = 0.749$, $p = 0.005$) for the ASD-LI group. Similar to the ASD-LI group, frame of mind references was significantly associated with a range of different linguistic measures produced during the narrative task for the DLD group: this includes the number of words ($r = 0.848$, $p = 0.001$), mean length of utterance ($r = 0.687$, $p = 0.020$), and the number of propositions ($r = 0.684$, $p = 0.020$). References to frames of mind were also associated with character speech ($r = 0.604$, $p = 0.049$) and negative propositions ($r = 0.684$, $p = 0.020$) for the DLD group. Like the ASD-LI group, the number of emotive terms used was significantly associated with the production of interjections during narrator speech for the DLD group ($r = 0.654$, $p = 0.029$). Finally, references to frames of mind were associated with the number of words produced during storytelling ($r = 0.719$, $p = 0.45$), and the number of propositions ($r = 0.731$, $p = 0.040$) for the TD group. No other associations were detected.

To summarise, references to frames of mind were associated with the number of words produced during the narrative task for the ASD, ASD-LI, DLD, and TD groups. Frames of mind references were associated with the number of propositions for the ASD-LI, DLD, and TD groups whereas this was not detected for the ASD group. However, the number of propositions was associated with emotive terms for the ASD and ASD-LI groups. Additionally, the number of propositions produced during the narrative task were associated with behavioural terms and character speech for the ASD-LI group. References to frames of mind were associated with a range of linguistic measures for the ASD-LI and DLD groups including the mean length of utterance, number of words, and propositions used during the narrative task. Also, frame of mind references was associated with causal statements for the ASD-LI group. Interestingly, interjections produced during narrator speech were associated with emotive terms for the ASD-LI group and frame of mind references for the DLD group.

8.4   Results from the Play Method

Recordings of play sessions were analysed according to the type and frequency of interjections produced by each participant. Four different categories of interjections were identified: cognitive, emotive, phatic, and volitive. The use of fillers was also included as a separate category as they provide an insight into a speaker's cognitive state. Examples of the types of interjections included within each category is provided in Figure 8 below.

Cognitive	Emotive	Phatic	Volitive	Filler
Aha	Ah	Hello	Look	Er
Eh	Argh	Mm	Wait	Hum
Huh	Aw	Uh-huh		Uh
	Come on!	Okay		Um
	Dammit!	Oh yeah		
	Eee!	Thank you		
	Finally!	Well done!		
	Gasp			
	God			
	Goodness me!			
	Grr!			
	Haha			
	Hey!			
	No!			
	Oh my God!			
	Oh well			
	Oi!			
	Oh no!			
	Ooh			
	Phew!			
	Please!			
	Really			
	Tut			
	Tsk			
	Ugh!			
	Uh oh!			
	Waa!			
	Wahoo!			
	What!			
	Whee!			
	Whoa!			
	Why			
	Wow			
	Yay!			
	Yes!			

Figure 8. A table showing the different types of interjections produced during the play session.

8.4.1   The Use of Cognitive Interjections

Cognitive interjections were not produced very often by all four groups during the play session, as demonstrated in Figure 9. To detect whether there were any significant group differences, the Kruskal-Wallis one-way ANOVA was used. This confirmed there were no significant group differences in regard to the use of cognitive interjections produced during the play session ($H(3) = 3.018$, $p = 0.389$). This finding is not surprising considering that cognitive interjections were used sparingly.

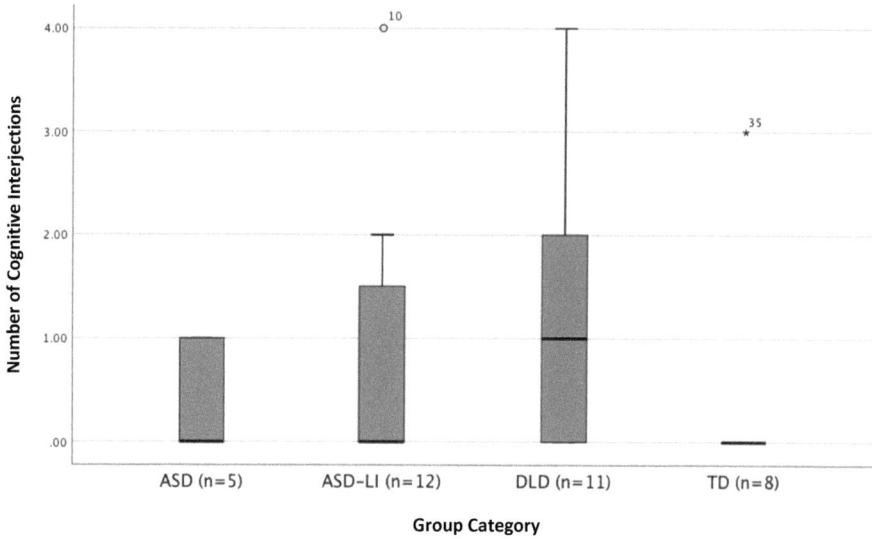

Figure 9. A box plot representing variation in the number of cognitive interjections produced during play, according to group category.

The non-parametric Spearman's Rho test was used to assess whether cognitive interjections were associated with any language measures. For the ASD-LI group, a significant association was found between cognitive interjections and CELF-5 Receptive Language Index scores ($r = 0.715$, $p = 0.009$) and Language Content scores ($r = 0.601$, $p = 0.039$). No other associations were found.

8.4.2 The Use of Emotive Interjections

Emotive interjections were used the most frequently during the play session, as closer inspection of Figure 10 reveals. Despite this, no significant group differences were detected in regard to the distribution of emotive interjections ($H(3) = 1.255, p = 0.740$). Further statistical tests were carried out to detect whether there were any discrepancies in the use of individual interjections. This revealed significant differences between groups in regard to the following interjections: *argh* ($H(3) = 8.375, p = 0.039$), *come on* ($H(3) = 14.649, p = 0.002$), and *grr* ($H(3) = 12.468, p = 0.006$). These findings were confirmed using the Kruskal-Wallis one-way ANOVA.

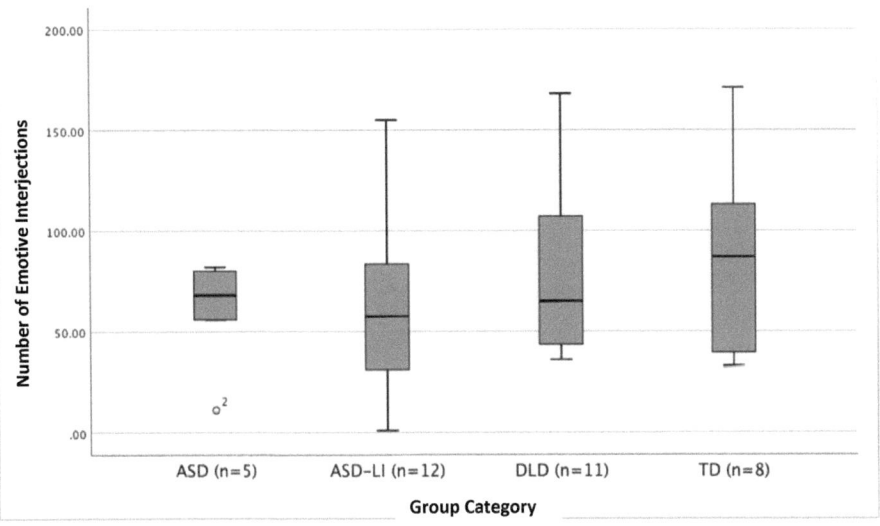

Figure 10. A box plot representing variation in the number of emotive interjections produced during the play session, according to group category.

Pairwise comparisons using the Bonferroni correction for multiple tests revealed that the DLD group produced *argh* significantly more than the TD group ($p = 0.047$). Also, the DLD group produced *grr* significantly more than the ASD-LI ($p = 0.015$) and the TD groups ($p = 0.044$). This did not reach significance levels with the ASD group. Further statistical tests, however, revealed that the ASD group produced *come on* significantly more than the ASD-LI ($p = 0.27$), DLD ($p = 0.007$), and the TD groups ($p = 0.004$).

Significant differences between groups were detected in regard to the distribution of *ha* ($H(3)$ = 12.230, p = 0.007) and *haha* ($H(3)$ = 11.243, p = 0.010). These findings were confirmed through using the Kruskal-Wallis one-way ANOVA. Pairwise comparisons revealed that the ASD-LI group produced *ha* significantly more than the TD group (p = 0.005). The contextual uses of *ha*, however, must be taken into consideration as this interjection was restricted in its production to express mockery when an opponent landed on a snake or lost a game. It must be noted that *haha* is an interjection used to represent laughter. The TD group produced *haha* significantly more than the ASD group (p = 0.048). This failed to reach significance levels when compared to the ASD-LI group (p = 0.097). Furthermore, the Kruskal-Wallis one-way ANOVA detected significant differences between groups in regard to the distribution of the following interjections: *oh my god* ($H(3) = 8.414$, $p = 0.038$), *really* ($H(3) = 8.474$, $p = 0.037$), and *yes* ($H(3) = 8.462$, $p = 0.037$). Pairwise comparisons, however, failed to detect any significant differences between groups. Next, the Spearman's Rho test was used to detect whether emotive interjections were associated with language measures. This revealed that emotive interjections were associated with the use of cognitive terms during the storytelling task for the ASD-LI group ($r = 0.704$, $p = 0.11$). No other group associations were detected.

8.4.3   The Use of Phatic Interjections

There were significant group differences in regard to the distribution of phatic interjections ($H(3) = 10.679$, $p = 0.014$), as the Kruskal-Wallis one-way ANOVA detected. Closer inspection of Figure 11 reveals that the mean number of phatic interjections for the ASD group is higher compared to the ASD-LI, DLD, and TD groups. Pairwise comparisons using the Bonferroni correction for multiple tests revealed that the ASD group produced significantly more phatic interjections than the DLD group ($H(3) = 10.679$, $p = 0.014$). No other group differences were detected.

To assess whether there were any discrepancies in the use of individual phatic interjections, the Kruskal-Wallis one-way ANOVA was conducted. This revealed that there were significant differences detected between groups in regard to the distribution of *okay* ($H(3) = 17.7442$, $p = 0.001$). Pairwise comparisons using the Bonferroni correction for multiple tests found that the TD group produced *okay* significantly more than the ASD-LI group ($p = 0.032$) and the DLD group ($p = 0.006$). The ASD and the TD group did not differ from one-another ($p = 1.000$). The

ASD group produced *okay* more than the ASD-LI ($p = 0.192$) and the DLD groups ($p = 0.052$), however it failed to reach significance levels.

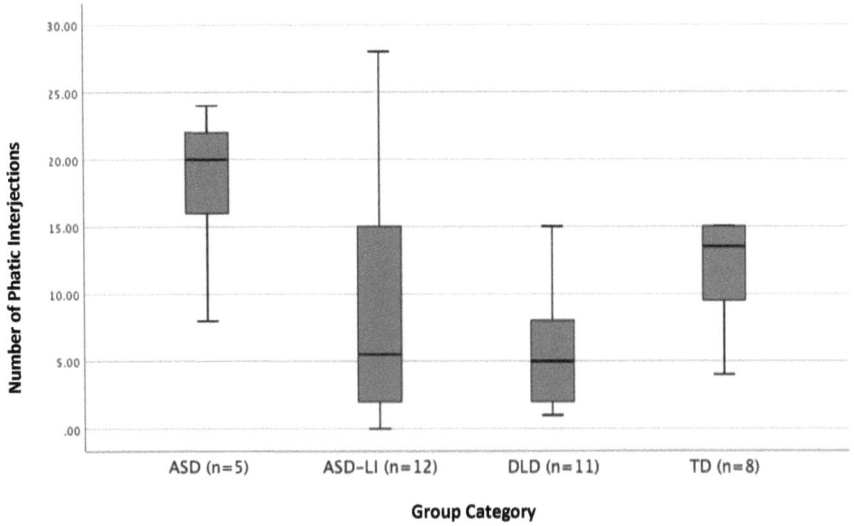

Figure 11. A box plot representing variation in the number of phatic interjections produced during the play session, according to group category.

The non-parametric Spearman's Rho test was used to assess whether phatic interjections were associated with a range of language measures. This test revealed that phatic interjections were in fact significantly associated with a range of different language measures including BPVS-3 raw scores ($r = 0.612$, $p = <0.001$) and all of the CELF-5 standardised language scores (Receptive Language Index: $r = 0.711$, $p = <0.001$; Expressive Language Index: $r = 0.526$, $p = 0.001$; Core Language Score: $r = 0.611$, $p = <0.001$, and Language Content Index: $r = 0.671$, $p = <0.001$). In addition to this, phatic interjections were significantly associated with a range of language measures used during the storytelling task including the following: the number of words ($r = 0.558$, $p = <0.001$), mean length of utterance ($r = 0.504$, $p = 0.002$), the number of propositions ($r = 0.391$, $p = 0.020$), references to frames of mind ($r = 0.407$, $p = 0.015$), cognitive terms ($r = 0.391$, $p = 0.020$), and character speech ($r = 0.443$, $p = 0.008$). Using this method, the Spearman's Rho test revealed that the use of phatic interjections was associated with age for the ASD group ($r = 0.900$, $p = 0.037$). However, it must be noted that the ASD group consisted of 1 child and 4 adolescents therefore this may have had an impact on the outcome. For the ASD-LI group, phatic interjections were significantly associated with CELF-5 Receptive Language Index scores ($r = 0.798$, $p = 0.002$) and Language Content Index scores ($r = 0.751$, $p = 0.005$). Also, phatic interjections were associated with the use of cognitive terms during the narrative task for the ASD-LI group ($r = 0.786$, $p = 0.002$). No other associations were detected. Given that phatic interjections are used to maintain social interaction, these findings exemplify the interrelation between linguistic abilities and communication.

8.4.4 The Use of Volitive Interjections

There were only two volitive interjections used amongst all four groups: these were *look* and *wait*. Closer inspection of Figure 12 reveals that the TD group produced the most volitive interjections whereas these were used sparingly by the DLD group. However, a Kruskal-Wallis one-way ANOVA revealed that there were no significant differences among groups in regard to the distribution of volitive interjections ($H(3) = 6.948$, $p = 0.074$).

The non-parametric Spearman's Rho test was used to assess whether volitive interjections were associated with a range of language measures. Although they were used sparingly, volitive interjections were significantly associated with a range of language measures including BPVS-3 raw scores ($r = 0.402$, $p = 0.017$) and all of the CELF-5 language measures (Receptive Language Index: $r = 0.574$, $p = {<}0.001$; Expressive Language Index; $r = 0.462$, $p = 0.005$; Core Language Score: $r = 0.517$, $p = 0.001$; Language Content Index: $r = 0.561$, $p = {<}0.001$). In addition to this, volitive interjections were associated with negative propositions used during the storytelling task ($r = 0.348$, $p = 0.040$).

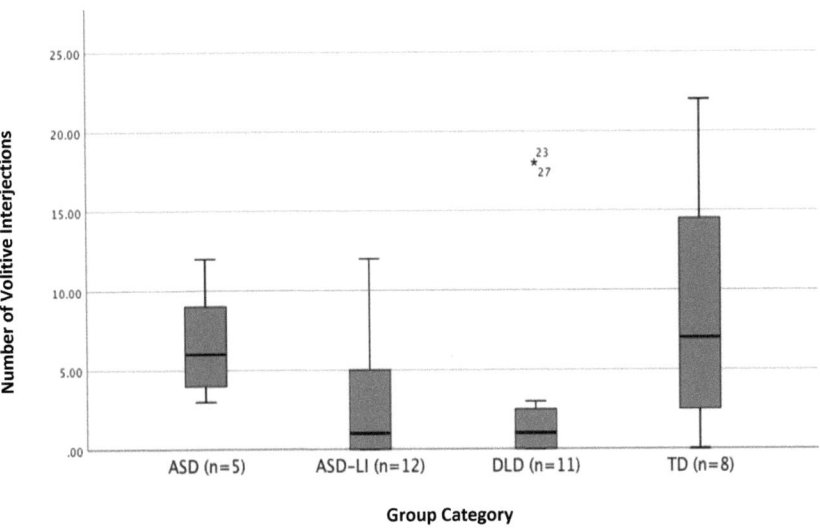

Figure 12. A box plot representing variation in the number of volitive interjections produced during the play session, according to group category.

8.4.5 The Use of Fillers

Fillers were included in this study as they provide an insight into a speaker's cognitive and linguistic state. Participants played snakes and ladders during this study, and the game involves conducting some basic calculations such as addition. Participants must also demonstrate an ability to understand the rules of the game and follow instructions, thus cognitive skills are required. Four fillers were chosen for investigation: *er, hum, uh,* and *um.*

Closer inspection of Figure 13 reveals that fillers were used sparingly by all four groups. Thus, groups did not differ from one-another significantly in regard to the distribution of fillers ($H(3) = 3.335, p = 0.343$), as the Kruskal-Wallis one-way ANOVA detected.

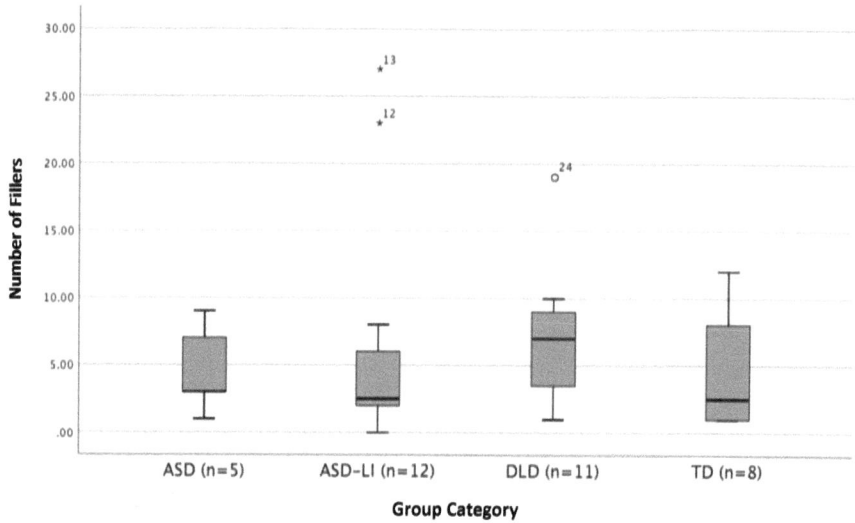

Figure 13. A box plot representing variation in the mean number of fillers produced during play, according to group category.

To assess whether there were any associations between the use of fillers, the Spearman's Rho test was conducted. For the ASD group, there was a negative correlation between the use of fillers and CELF-5 Core Language Scores and Receptive Language Index scores (both values are $r = -0.975$, $p = 0.005$). No other differences were detected.

8.5 Summary of Results

Analysis of linguistic abilities during the narrative task revealed that the DLD group produced significantly fewer words and fewer propositions in comparison to the TD cohort. While generating a story using the picture book *Hug*, the ASD, ASD-LI, and TD groups did not differ from one-another when the number of propositions was calculated. Additionally, the utterances produced by the DLD group were significantly shorter compared to those produced by the ASD and TD groups. Auxiliary omissions and agreement errors were made by the DLD group significantly more compared to the ASD group. This failed to reach significance levels with the ASD-LI group and, more surprisingly, the TD group. Groups did not differ from one-another in regard to the number of over-regularisations, omission of determiners, and pronoun errors made during the narrative task. Surprisingly, no significant differences were detected between groups in regard to the number of frames of mind references produced during the narrative task: this includes emotive terms, behavioural references, and cognitive terms. Also, groups did not differ in regard to the number of causal statements, hedges, and negative propositions produced. The DLD group, however, used character speech significantly less than the TD group during the story generation task. It is worth noting that the DLD group used fewer instances of character speech compared to the ASD group, however this narrowly missed reaching significance levels. Interestingly, the ASD group produced significantly more emotive interjections during non-narrator speech compared to the ASD-LI group. Although the ASD group produced more emotive interjections compared to the TD cohort during non-narrator speech, this failed to reach significance levels. Interjectional usage during character speech in the narrative task was minimal, thus no group differences were detected. Analysis of narrative performance revealed that the DLD group required significantly more prompts by the researcher compared to the ASD, ASD-LI, and TD groups. The DLD group also produced significantly more fillers than the ASD-LI group while telling a story. No other differences were detected.

During the play session, **cognitive interjections** were used sparingly by all four groups. Cognitive interjections were, however, associated with CELF-5 Receptive Language Index and Language Content scores for the ASD-LI group. Similarly, **emotive interjections** were used sparingly during the play session; consequently, no group differences were found. Nevertheless, discrepancies between groups were detected in the use of individual interjections. For example, the DLD group produced *argh* significantly more than the TD group. Also, the DLD group produced *grr* significantly more than the ASD-LI and TD groups. This did not reach significance levels with the ASD group. Further statistical tests, however, revealed that the ASD group produced *come on* significantly more than the ASD-LI, DLD, and the TD groups. Emotive interjections were associated with the use of cognitive terms during the storytelling task for the ASD-LI group.

Interestingly, the ASD group produced significantly more **phatic interjections** compared to the DLD group during the play session. Phatic interjections were associated with a range of different language measures including BPVS-3 raw scores and all of the CELF-5 sub-tests. Phatic interjections were also significantly associated with a range of language measures used during the storytelling task including the following: the number of words, mean length of utterance, the number of propositions, references to frames of mind, cognitive terms, and character speech. For the ASD-LI group, phatic interjections were significantly associated with CELF-5 Receptive Language Index scores and Language Content Index scores. Also, an association was detected between the use of phatic interjections during the play session and cognitive terms produced during the narrative task for the ASD-LI group.

Volitive interjections were used sparingly during the play session by all four groups. Despite this, an association was detected between the use of volitive interjections during play, BPVS-3 raw scores, and all of the CELF-5 language measures. Volitive interjections were also associated with the use of negative propositions during the story generation task. Finally, no group differences were detected in regard to the use of fillers during the play session. For the ASD group, a negative correlation was detected between the use of fillers during play, CELF-5 Core Language scores, and Receptive Language Index scores. No other differences were detected.

Overall, the results from this study exemplify the remarkable differences between the ASD and the ASD-LI groups performance on a number of linguistic measures. While the ASD group demonstrated notable similarities to the TD group, the ASD-LI groups performance during the narrative task bore more resemblances to the DLD group. These findings demonstrate the presence of a language impairment, whether co-occurring with ASD or on its own in the form of DLD, leads to similar performance in the tasks used in the current study. Moreover, the results from this study reveal that interjectional usage is closely related to language ability. The prevalence of ASD has little effect on interjectional usage, and this is apparent as both the ASD and ASD-LI groups used a range of cognitive, emotive, phatic, and volitive interjections during both the narrative task and the play session. The next chapter moves on to discuss the findings of this study in further detail.

Chapter 9. Discussion

This study measured the linguistic abilities of children and adolescents with Autism Spectrum Disorder (ASD), Autism Spectrum Disorder with an accompanying language impairment (ASD-LI), Developmental Language Disorder (DLD), and a typically developing (TD) cohort. This was achieved through conducting the British Picture Vocabulary Scale – Third Edition (BPVS-3, Dunn *et al.*, 2009) and the Clinical Evaluation of Language Fundamentals – Fifth Edition (CELF-5, Wiig *et al.*, 2017) with all participants, and comparisons were drawn between all four groups in regard to performance during the aforementioned clinical assessments. The BPVS-3 (Dunn *et al.*, 2009) is a standardised assessment used to measure receptive vocabulary. Participants are presented with four images on each page and, upon hearing the administrator utter the test word, they must select one corresponding image through providing a verbal response or gesturing towards their chosen answer. The CELF-5 (Wiig *et al.*, 2017) is a standardised assessment used to identify, diagnose, and provide an evaluation of a person's overall language abilities. The CELF-5 (Wiig *et al.*, 2017) provides an insight into a person's receptive and expressive language skills, core language abilities, and language use in relation to content. The distinction between them is as follows: receptive language assesses comprehension and listening, expressive scores measure oral language expression, core language scores measure a person's overall language ability, and language content is a measurement of a person's vocabulary and world knowledge. A narrative task was included in this study which involved participant's generating a story using the picture book *Hug* by Jez Alborough (2000). The first two pages of the book were narrated to participants and they were then instructed to continue telling the rest of the story. This format was formerly used in Siller *et al.*'s (2014) study. Comparisons were drawn between all four groups in regard to linguistic and narrative abilities, as well as interjectional usage. Spontaneous speech was elicited through playing the board game snakes and ladders with participants one-to-one, and this proved to be more fruitful in eliciting interjections compared to the narrative task. This finding should be borne in mind if further research into interjectional usage were to take place. One plausible explanation for this outcome is that the board game allowed for more opportunities for the spontaneous elicitation of interjections due to the unpredictable and competitive nature of the game. Also, the board game provided an opportunity for dialogue between the researcher and participants whereas the narrative task was carried out independently. This should be taken into consideration as interjections often feature in spoken discourse.

Firstly, this study was successful in exemplifying notable similarities and differences between all four groups. To begin with, parallels between the ASD and ASD-LI groups will be explored. Although the mean CELF-5 Core Language score for the ASD group was higher than that of the ASD-LI group, the groups did not differ from one another significantly. This outcome had not been predicted. Core language scores are a measurement of overall language ability, and scores are based upon performance during four sub-tests: formulating sentences, recalling sentences, understanding spoken paragraphs, and semantic relationships. A plausible explanation for this unexpected finding is that both the ASD and the ASD-LI cohorts exhibited difficulties during the understanding spoken paragraphs sub-test. This task involves listening to a number of paragraphs, uttered by the examiner, and they are then assessed on their ability to answer a number of questions in relation to what they heard and understood. The understanding spoken paragraphs sub-test of the CELF-5 (Wiig *et al.*, 2017) involves identifying cause and effect relationships, as well as making inferences and predictions. As stated in the literature review, previous studies have established that theory of mind is an impairment in ASD (Baron-Cohen *et al.*, 1985; Happé, 1995; Losh and Capps, 2003; Tager-Flusberg, 2011). Theory of mind is a fundamental part of communication as it can be used to formulate inferences and make predictions about another person's behaviour, as well as allowing for the interpretation of other people's actions (Premack and Woodruff, 1978; Happé, 1994; Tager-Flusberg and Sullivan, 1995). Taking this into consideration, it can be plausibly suggested that the understanding spoken paragraphs sub-test of the CELF-5 may be difficult for individuals with ASD, regardless of their receptive and expressive language abilities being in-tact. This proposal can be used as a possible explanation for why there were no significant differences detected between the ASD and the ASD-LI groups core language scores.

On the other hand, notable discrepancies between the ASD and ASD-LI groups were exemplified in this study. This is an important finding as it recognises distinctions between the two groups. Also, it provides scope to the argument that individuals with ASD should be subdivided into those who do have an accompanying language impairment (ASD-LI) and those with normal language skills in research studies. In the present study, the ASD group obtained significantly higher mean BPVS-3 raw scores than the ASD-LI group, and the former outperformed the ASD-LI group when they were assessed on their receptive, expressive, and language content abilities using the CELF-5. Throughout this book, emphasis has been placed upon the importance of making these categorical divisions in future research as it allows for a greater insight into the cognitive and linguistic abilities of individuals with ASD and ASD-LI.

Prior studies have tended to subsume individuals with autism under one category, and many studies have not made the distinction between those with and without a language impairment. The results from this study demonstrate that language impairment, which is comorbid with ASD in the ASD-LI group, has an effect on the tasks administered.

This study was effective in highlighting remarkable similarities between the ASD-LI and the DLD groups, particularly when they were assessed on their language abilities. Firstly, the groups did not differ significantly from one-another when their mean BPVS-3 raw scores were calculated. Unlike the ASD group, both the ASD-LI and the DLD groups performed significantly worse than the TD group when their mean BPVS-3 raw scores were calculated. Secondly, the ASD-LI and the DLD groups did not differ significantly from one-another when they were assessed on their receptive and expressive language abilities, as well as core language and language index scores. These were measured using the CELF-5. Unlike the ASD group, the ASD-LI and DLD groups performed significantly worse than the TD group when they were assessed on all four language measures using the CELF-5. The findings from this study exemplify the alikeness between the two groups, hereby providing scope for further research to investigate the similarities of ASD-LI and DLD. As it stands, ASD and DLD are classed as two distinct neurodevelopmental disorders. However, it is plausible to suggest that neurological similarities may account for the notable similarities in language performance between the ASD-LI and the DLD cohorts. Previous research, for example, has reported that children with autism and an accompanying language impairment and children with Specific Language Impairment had reversed rightward asymmetry in the inferior frontal gyrus and significant asymmetry of the planum temporale (De Fossé *et al.*, 2004, p. 762).

Quite remarkably, this study was successful in highlighting notable similarities between the ASD and the TD groups performance on a number of language measures. The ASD group did not differ from the TD group when they were assessed on their receptive vocabulary abilities using the BPVS-3, nor did the groups differ from one-another when they were assessed on all CELF-5 measures. This includes receptive language, expressive language, core language, and language content scores. These findings had not been predicted. Thus, further research investigating the neurological underpinnings of language in individuals with ASD and a typically developing cohort is warranted. Interestingly, a previous study conducted by De Fossé *et al.* (2004, p. 762) found that children with autism and normal language skills and typically developing children had similar leftward volumetric asymmetry of the inferior frontal gyrus, pars opercularis and pars triangularis. These regions of the brain are associated with Broca's area which controls the production of language. It must be noted that the chronological ages of the ASD cohort were higher than the TD group in this study, thus it would be insightful if the two groups were matched accordingly in future research projects. Nevertheless, age was accounted for in the results through using multiple regression modelling.

9.1 Findings from the Narrative Task

Narrative abilities will be closely examined in this section of the book. Interestingly, groups did not differ from one-another in regard to the number of utterances produced during the storytelling task in the current study. This outcome is contrary to that of Capps *et al.* (2000) and Siller *et al.* (2000) who found that children with ASD used fewer utterances than typically developing children. Throughout the story, there were many instances of the word *hug* used in the picture book therefore this may have aided participants during the story generation task. For example, there was a tendency for children with DLD to utter many instances of *hug* whereby they were in fact reading the word aloud rather than embedding it within a proposition. This explains why there were no significant differences detected between the groups in regard to the number of utterances produced. Surprisingly, no significant differences were detected between the ASD, ASD-LI, and TD groups in regard to the number of words produced during the narrative task. This finding is contrary to that of Siller *et al.* (2014) who found that children with ASD used fewer words than typically developing children during narrative production. As previously stated, the fact that the book contained numerous instances of the word *hug* may have aided participants while generating a story. Significantly fewer words were produced by the DLD group during the storytelling task in comparison to the typically developing cohort. This is not surprising given that the CELF-5 Expressive Language Index scores for the DLD group were significantly lower than the TD group, and that a diagnosis of Language Disorder is based upon production and/or comprehension deficits. One interesting finding from this study is that although the DLD group produced fewer words than the ASD and ASD-LI groups, pairwise comparisons using the Bonferroni correction for multiple tests found that these results were not statistically significant.

Significantly fewer propositions were produced by the DLD group compared to the typically developing cohort. This is in line with previous studies as both Kaderavek and Sulzby (2000) and Reilly *et al.* (2004) found that children with SLI produced shorter stories than typically developing children. Difficulties with expressive language skills, characteristic of a Language Disorder, may have inhibited those individuals from being able to produce longer, complex, and more detailed narratives. As previously stated in the methodology chapter of this book, propositions are defined as a complete phrase consisting of a verb and its arguments (Botting, 2002). A single proposition must therefore contain a minimum of one verb and one noun (Botting, 2002). With regard to semantics, one proposition typically equates to a single event (Capps *et al.*, 2000). During the storytelling task, the DLD group tended to focus more upon uttering the word *hug* as opposed to embodying it within a proposition, hence why they used significantly fewer propositions compared to the other three groups. Calculating the total number of propositions is a useful tool used to measure narrative length. Interestingly, the ASD, ASD-LI, and the TD groups did not differ from one-another significantly in regard to the number of propositions produced during the storytelling task. This finding is consistent with that of Losh and Capps (2003), as they found no differences between the length of narratives produced by children with ASD and typically developing children.

Language Disorder is diagnosed according to comprehension and/or production deficits. The DLD group produced significantly more agreement errors than the ASD group, however it is somewhat surprising that this failed to reach statistical significance levels compared to the TD group. Nevertheless, the DLD group produced more agreement errors than the TD group. This is in line with Norbury and Bishop's (2003) findings that children with SLI make more grammatical tense errors compared to typically developing children. The mean chronological age of the ASD group was higher than the typically developing cohort in this study, thus the groups were not matched accordingly as difficulties arose during the recruitment process. The difference in chronological ages of the groups may have influenced the results to a degree. For example, the ASD group was composed of 1 primary-school aged child and 4 secondary school pupils whereas the typically developing cohort was solely made up of 8 primary-school aged children. Considering that the ASD group were predominantly made up of secondary school pupils, it is plausible to suggest that they are less likely to make agreement errors through having experienced a longer period of time accessing formal education. Also, language skills were not impaired in the ASD group.

Previous studies investigating interjectional usage have based their findings on transcripts of spoken discourse obtained from an online database. This preliminary study advances upon prior studies as it is the first to use a narrative task to investigate interjectional usage. By doing so, it offers an insight into narrator's abilities to express characters internal mental states through the use of interjections. This is a component of theory of mind. The narrative procedure provided an insight into participants emotion recognition abilities through being able to correctly identify characters emotions, taking the context into consideration. Also, the narrative task provided an insight into participants theory of mind abilities through the production of character speech and references to frames of mind. Thus, an emotion recognition and a false-belief task was not included in the present study as an indication into participants abilities could be obtained through the narrative procedure. It may be beneficial, however, if future studies incorporated emotion recognition and theory of mind tasks to explore the relationship further.

False-belief tasks and Happe's (1994) *Strange Stories* are the most well-known tools for assessing a person's theory of mind abilities, although individuals need to have a certain degree of linguistic proficiency to be able to meet the demands of the tasks. For example, participants must be able to understand and respond to questions asked by the researcher. Consequently, individuals with a severe language impairment are often unable to partake as they do not possess the language and/or cognitive skills required to meet the demands. Interjections, however, are independent from the syntactic rules governing a language and they are not embedded by the grammar of a clause (Ameka, 1992; Wharton, 2009). Thus, interjections can function as standalone utterances. One unanticipated finding from this study was that there were no significant differences between all four groups in regard to the number of references to frames of mind produced during the storytelling task. This outcome is in line with a number of previous studies which have also reported no significant differences in internal state language use, produced during storytelling tasks, by children with ASD and typically developing children (Norbury and Bishop, 2003; Norbury *et al.*, 2014; Banney *et al.*, 2015). For clarification purposes, the term frames of mind can be interchangeable with internal state language. To detect whether there were any distinctions between the groups, references to frames of mind were sub-divided into the following: emotive, behavioural, and cognitive terms. Surprisingly, no differences were found between the groups in regard to the number of emotive, behavioural, and cognitive terms produced during the storytelling task. These findings are in line with previous studies which have reported that children with ASD are as proficient as their typically developing peers at incorporating emotion terms within their narratives (Tager-Flusberg and Sullivan, 1995; Norbury and Bishop, 2003; Banney *et al.*, 2015), as well as referring to characters cognitive states (Tager-Flusberg and Sullivan, 1995; Capps *et al.*, 2000; Norbury and Bishop, 2003; Siller *et al.*, 2014; Banney *et al.*, 2015). Simple emotions, such as *happy* and *sad*, were contained within the picture book *Hug*, therefore it may have been difficult to elicit more complex emotions based on the plot. Also, the vast majority of participants correctly identified that the monkey was sad which was illustrated through Bobo crying while sat down on a rock. Most participants also recognised Bobo's happy emotional state when he was finally reunited with his mother. Previous studies have found that children with autism or Asperger's Syndrome (AS) are as capable as typically developing children at recognising facial expressions depicting the six basic emotions (Castelli, 2005). In Castelli's (2005) study, participants were assessed on their abilities to match standardised photographic images of facial expressions, depicting various emotions at different intensity levels, to an appropriate emotion label. The emotions used were happiness, anger, surprise, disgust, fear, and sadness; these are the six universal states listed under the basic theory of emotion. Emotion recognition deficits, however, seem to be more apparent when high-functioning individuals with ASD are assessed on their ability to recognise more complex emotions (Heaton *et al.*, 2012). With this in mind, it is plausible to suggest that the children and adolescents with ASD and ASD-LI included in this study were proficient in being able to detect the emotional expressions depicted upon characters faces within the storybook.

Cognitive references were used sparingly by all four groups during the narrative task. One possible explanation for this finding may be that the picture book *Hug* did not provide many opportunities for the elicitation of cognitive terms as it was orientated more towards the emotions experienced by the protagonist Bobo. Surprisingly, no significant differences were detected between individual groups use of causal statements during the storytelling task. This outcome is contrary to that of Losh and Capps (2003), who found that typically developing children produced significantly more causal statements than children with autism or AS during two narrative procedures: telling a personal narrative and generating a story using a wordless picture book. However, Losh and Capps' (2003) results from the narrative tasks were used collectively therefore it cannot be deciphered whether there were any discrepancies in the use of causal statements between the two tasks. Another notable finding from the current study is that the DLD group used character speech significantly less than the TD group. Character speech is a form of perspective taking as it requires the narrator to put themselves in the characters position. The ability to do so relates to theory of mind, and this is concerned with the ability to recognise one's own internal mental state as well as identify and attribute mental states to other people. Theory of mind abilities are a crucial element of character speech as a narrator must be able to infer characters internal states including their thoughts, feelings, and emotions, and apply context to provide an appropriate response. Interestingly, the DLD group did not differ from the ASD-LI group in regard to the use of character speech during the narrative task. The ASD group produced more instances of character speech compared to the DLD group, however this just failed to reach significance levels. No other group differences were detected.

Although interjections were used sparingly by all four groups during the narrative task, one interesting finding worthy of mention is that the ASD, ASD-LI, and DLD groups incorporated interjections within character speech. This exemplifies that interjections can be used not only to express a speaker's internal mental state, but also it is applicable to others. This finding contradicts Stange's (2016) claim that interjections are typically used to express one's own mental state and not those of other people. Thus, it can be suggested that interjections used in this context relate to theory of mind abilities. To date, there are no studies investigating interjections and theory of mind therefore this may be a fruitful topic for further research. This finding was unexpected considering that theory of mind is an impairment in ASD (Baron-Cohen *et al.*, 1985; Happé, 1995; Losh and Capps, 2003; Tager-Flusberg, 2011). Surprisingly, the TD children did not produce any inter-jections during character speech. Interjections, however, were incorporated into non-narrator speech by all four groups, and examples include stepping out of the narrator role to ask questions or making commentaries about the story such as '*Ah, this is quite sad.*' This finding exemplifies that interjections are a natural part of spoken discourse and they are therefore worthy of further research. With regard to the number of prompts required during the storytelling task, the DLD group required significantly more encouragement which was essential for the continuation of their narratives when compared to the ASD, ASD-LI, and TD groups. These results are consistent with those of Wetherell *et al.* (2007) who found that adolescents with SLI required significantly more prompts than their typically developing peers during the production of spontaneous narratives and during a storytelling task using a wordless picture book. Another notable finding from this study is that the DLD group produced more fillers than the ASD-LI group although no other group differences were detected. Fillers provide an insight into a person's cognitive and linguistic abilities. Frequent use of fillers, for example, in this context may be indicative of a narrator's difficulty interpreting the images depicted in the picture book. Also, frequent use of fillers can express a speaker's difficulty in formulating an utterance. Although fillers are a natural part of spoken discourse, there is a tendency for researchers to omit them from study when investigating narrative abilities as they focus more upon the linguistic elements produced instead.

9.2 Findings from the Play Method

Previous studies investigating interjections have based their findings upon analysing transcripts of spoken discourse, such as in Asano's (1997) and Stange's (2016) study. With regard to the latter, Stange (2016) investigated the use of interjections by children during play sessions. Similarly, the current study incorporated play to investigate the use of interjections within a naturalistic context. The benefit of using this method is that it provides an insight into natural language use as exclamations were uttered spontaneously.

Cognitive interjections were used sparingly during the play session therefore no differences were detected between groups. While playing the board game snakes and ladders, there may not have been many opportunities for a speaker to express their cognitive state. Only three cognitive interjections were used throughout: *aha, eh*, and *huh*. According to the Oxford English Dictionary, *aha* is an interjection typically used to express sudden realisation whereas *eh* and *huh* are used interrogatively as a request for the repetition or explanation of something which has just been said. Cognitive interjections can therefore be uttered to indicate difficulties in processing information, such as a speaker's utterance, or a confused state of mind. Interestingly, cognitive interjections were associated with CELF-5 Receptive Language Index and Language Content Index scores for the ASD-LI group. This finding, while preliminary, can be used to suggest that individuals with lower receptive language abilities may produce cognitive interjections to express uncertainty more frequently than individuals with normal language skills. Further research, however, is required to support this claim.

Emotive interjections convey the emotions and sensations that a speaker experiences at a given time. Some examples of emotive interjections uttered during the play session were *yay*, *wow*, and *oh no!* Stange (2016) used transcripts of recorded children's play sessions in her investigation into emotive interjections in British English. In Stange's (2016) study, the following emotive interjections were investigated: *ow, ouch, ugh, yuck, whoops, whoopsa-daisy,* and *wow*. This preliminary study advances upon Stange's (2016) investigation through providing a broader scope of emotive interjections used during the play session, as outlined in Figure 8. Interestingly, emotive interjections were produced the most frequently during the play session. The unpredictable and competitive nature of the game is a plausible explanation for this finding; as two players compete to win, emotions may be heightened. Surprisingly, no significant differences were reported between groups in regard to the distribution of emotive interjections during spontaneous play. This finding contradicts my prediction that the ASD and ASD-LI groups will produce fewer emotive interjections than the DLD and TD groups during the play session. Furthermore, this result indicates that individuals with ASD and ASD-LI are as proficient as individuals with DLD and typically developing individuals at expressing their own emotional states. Prior research into emotion, however, has focused more upon recognition rather than expression (Scherer, 1986; Keltner and Ekman, 2003; Goddard, 2014). Given that interjections are defined as utterances used to express emotion, they may be a fruitful topic for future research studies within this field. This study is a preliminary investigation into emotional expression in ASD, ASD-LI, DLD, and typical development. All four groups produced interjections to express their own internal states. There is abundant room for further research to expand upon this. By doing so, the findings can help determine whether there are apparent discrepancies in the use of emotional expressions between these groups and other clinical populations. In the same vein, closer examination revealed that there were discrepancies between groups in regard to interjectional usage. For example, the DLD group produced *argh* significantly more than the TD group. *Argh* is an interjection which is typically uttered to express disappointment and frustration. In addition to this, the DLD group produced *grr* significantly more than the ASD-LI and the TD group. *Grr* is an interjection typically used to express anger. One notable finding from the study is that there were no differences reported between the DLD and the ASD groups in regard to the use of *grr* during the spontaneous play task. Similarly, *come on* is an interjection used to express anger or frustration. The ASD group were found to produce *come on* significantly more than the other three groups. Meanwhile, the ASD-LI group produced *ha* significantly more than the TD children. As stated in the previous chapter, the interjection *ha* was used mockingly in the event of the researcher landing on a snake or having lost a game. On the other hand, TD children produced more instances of laughter, represented by the interjection *haha*, than the ASD and ASD-LI groups. Despite this, the Kruskal-Wallis one-way ANOVA showed that these results were not statistically significant. Another notable finding is that emotive interjections were associated with the use of cognitive terms during the storytelling task for the ASD-LI group.

Phatic interjections are typically used to maintain social communication and some examples include *mm, okay*, and *uh-huh*. Previous studies have regarded interjections as not being an integral part of language. However, the current study found that phatic interjections were associated with BPVS-3 raw scores and all of the CELF-5 sub-tests. Phatic interjections were also associated with a range of linguistic measures including the number of words produced during the storytelling task, mean length of utterance, number of propositions, internal state language, and character speech. In the Diagnostic and Statistical Manual of Mental Disorders – Fifth Edition (DSM-5, American Psychiatric Association, 2013), Autism Spectrum Disorder and Language Disorder are both classed as communication disorders. Contrary to expectations, the ASD group produced significantly more phatic interjections compared to the DLD group during the play session. One notable finding from the current study was that the ASD, ASD-LI, and TD groups did not differ from one another in regard to their use of phatic interjections. This finding was unexpected considering that phatic interjections are used to maintain social communication and this forms one of the triad of impairments in ASD. Together, these findings indicate that the use of phatic interjections is related to language ability rather than prevalence of ASD. The present study involved the researcher visiting numerous schools in the North East and working with participants in the classroom context. Play sessions are incorporated within the school environment, and all participants were familiar with the game snakes and ladders. This was confirmed through the researcher asking each participant if they had played the game before prior to starting. There are many advantages of play sessions as they provide an opportunity for children to learn turn-taking skills, develop communication skills, and interact with others. With this in mind, speech and language therapists often incorporate play within the sessions they undertake with children as it provides an opportunity for them to teach the aforementioned skills.

Volitive interjections are used to convey a person wanting something in the semantic meaning of their utterance; an example of this would be the English interjection *ssh!* Volitive interjections were used sparingly during the play session, although there may not have been many opportunities to elicit volitive interjections given the nature of the game. There were only two types of volitive interjections produced: *look* and *wait.* No significant differences were detected between groups in regard to the use of volitive interjections. However, it is worth noting that volitive interjections were associated with BPVS-3 raw scores and all CELF-5 language measures.

Fillers are sounds or words produced by a speaker to indicate a pause or hesitation during discourse and some examples include *er, hum, uh,* and *um.* Fillers provide an insight into a speaker's cognitive and linguistic state. No group differences were detected in the use of fillers during the play session. Interestingly, a negative correlation was detected between the use of fillers and CELF-5 Core Language Scores and Receptive Language Index scores for the ASD group. During spoken discourse, fillers can indicate a speaker's difficulty in processing information or formulating an utterance. Given that there was a negative correlation between receptive language scores and the use of fillers, it can be plausibly suggested that the ASD group were not subject to comprehension difficulties. No other associations were detected.

Chapter 10. Conclusion

This study set out with the aim of investigating the linguistic abilities of children and adolescents with Autism Spectrum Disorder (ASD), Autism Spectrum Disorder and an accompanying language impairment (ASD-LI), Developmental Language Disorder (DLD), and a typically developing (TD) cohort. Language impairment was confirmed if an individual obtained a value of 77 or below (-1.5 *SD* below the mean) on their receptive, expressive, or core language index score using the Clinical Evaluation of Language Fundamentals – Fifth Edition (CELF-5, Wiig *et al.*, 2017). Interestingly, the current study found that the ASD and TD groups performed on a similar level when their language abilities were assessed using the British Picture Vocabulary Scale – Third Edition (BPVS-3, Dunn *et al.*, 2009) and the CELF-5 (Wiig *et al.*, 2017). The research undertaken in this study has also exemplified the remarkable similarities between the ASD-LI and DLD groups in regard to their language abilities. For example, the ASD-LI and DLD groups did not differ from one-another in regard to BPVS-3 raw scores and performance during all CELF-5 measures. There is a tendency for researchers to subsume individuals with ASD under one category, and often researchers recruit individuals with high-functioning autism due to the accessibility and requirements of some tasks. A major advantage of distinguishing between ASD and ASD-LI in the current study is that it allowed for the detection of any discrepancies between the two groups, as detailed in this book.

The second aim is in fact the focal point of this study, which is to investigate the use of interjections by children and adolescents with ASD, ASD-LI, DLD, and a TD cohort. Interjections were elicited during spoken language, and this was successfully achieved through instructing participants to generate a story using a picture book and spontaneous play. The latter proved to be more fruitful in eliciting interjections, therefore this method may be useful if future research into this topic of investigation were to take place. Notwithstanding these limitations, the narrative procedure yielded interesting results. For example, no significant differences were detected between the groups in regard to frames of mind references including the use of cognitive, emotive, and behavioural terms. This finding may be due to the small number of participants who partook in the study; thus, it would be useful to replicate the study with a larger sample to see if the same result emerged. One of the more notable findings to emerge from this study is that interjections were used during character speech in the narrative task by the ASD, ASD-LI, and DLD groups. This was not reported for the typically developing cohort. This finding is noteworthy as character speech involves perspective taking as a narrator must imagine themselves being in someone else's position to understand their thoughts and feelings. By doing so, the narrator attributes mental states to the character and this cognitive ability concerns theory of mind. Previous studies have found that theory of mind is an impairment in ASD. The findings from this preliminary study indicate that individuals with ASD and ASD-LI are able to attribute mental states to other people, exemplified through incorporating interjections within character speech. With this in mind, it would be useful if future studies included narrative tasks within their investigation into interjectional usage as there is the potential for this approach to be fruitful in expanding our current understanding of the subject.

This study has been consistent in arguing that interjections are a crucial part of language, and their significance can be exemplified through interjections being among the first words acquired from birth. Interjections play an important role in early language development as they allow for a speaker to communicate their mental states without necessarily having fully mastered the syntactic, phonological, morphological, semantic, and pragmatic rules underpinning language. The significance of interjections can also be exemplified through their ability to function as holophrastic utterances which means they are able to express the same communicative content as longer, more complex utterances. To date, the study of interjections has been neglected and the number of studies investigating this topic is scarce. Thus, further research into the topic is warranted. The significance of this study can be exemplified through it being the first investigation into the use of interjections by individuals with ASD, ASD-LI, and DLD compared to a typically developing cohort. The present study is also the first comprehensive investigation into the use of interjections which adopts the narrative procedure as prior studies having based their findings upon transcripts of spoken discourse. For example, Asano (1997) and Stange (2016) sourced transcripts of spoken discourse during parent-child interactions from the Child Language Data Exchange System to conduct their investigations into interjectional usage. It is worth highlighting that both Asano and Stange were not present at the time of the recordings, therefore the findings from their studies were based upon inferences formed by taking the available contextual information into consideration. One advantage of the current study is that the researcher conducted tasks with participants first-hand therefore the context was known. This is significant considering that interjections are bound by context. The results from this study therefore provide a new insight into how interjections are used during storytelling, and the study lays the groundwork for future research. Also, the significance of this study can be further exemplified through it being the first of its kind to investigate interjectional usage among individuals with ASD, ASD-LI, DLD, and a TD cohort. One important finding from this study is that the ASD, ASD-LI, and TD groups did not differ in regard to their use of phatic interjections. This is noteworthy considering that phatic interjections are used to maintain social communication, and this forms one of the triad of impairments in ASD. Taking this into consideration, it can be plausibly suggested that inter-jectional usage is related to language ability rather than prevalence of ASD.

Another prominent finding from this study, which had not been predicted, is that interjections were associated with a range of linguistic abilities. For example, phatic interjections were significantly associated with a range of different language measures including BPVS-3 raw scores and all of the CELF-5 sub-tests: this includes Receptive Language Index, Expressive Language Index, Core Language Score, and Language Content Index. In addition to this, phatic interjections were significantly associated with a range of language measures used during the storytelling task including the following: the number of words, mean length of utterance, the number of propositions, references to frames of mind, cognitive terms, and character speech. In addition to this, volitive interjections were significantly associated with a range of language measures including BPVS-3 raw scores and all of the CELF-5 language measures including Receptive Language Index, Expressive Language Index, Core Language Score and Language Content Index. These findings emerged despite the fact that volitive interjections were used sparingly.

Associations were detected in regard to the type of interjections produced during tasks and group category. For the ASD-LI group, a significant association was found between the use of cognitive interjections during the play session and CELF-5 Receptive Language Index and Language Content scores. Also, cognitive interjections produced during narrator speech were associated with CELF-5 Receptive Language Index scores for the ASD-LI group. In addition, emotive interjections during character speech were associated with the number of utterances produced during the narrative task for the ASD-LI group. Phatic interjections were associated with the use of cognitive terms during the story generation task for the ASD-LI group. Like the ASD-LI group, the number of emotive terms used was significantly associated with the production of interjections during character speech for the DLD group. Emotive interjections were associated with CELF-5 Receptive Language Index and Language Content scores for the DLD group. Also, emotive interjections were associated with emotion terms used during the narrative task for the DLD group, as well as character speech.

This preliminary study has advanced upon prior studies investigating interjectional usage as it has been successful in demonstrating that interjections are an integral part of language, achieved through incorporating a range of language assessments such as the BPVS-3 and CELF-5. This finding should not be underestimated as the current study is the first to report on the intrinsic link between interjectional usage and language abilities. The study of interjections has been neglected by linguists to date. Consequently, there is the possibility that interjections may have been omitted from transcripts of spoken discourse as researchers tend to focus on the linguistic elements. Thus, interjections may have been omitted from storytelling transcripts; this is noteworthy considering that characters internal mental states can be expressed through the use of emotion terms but also interjections. This study has been successful in demonstrating that interjections can be used to express another person's mental state, as well as one's own. This is a component of theory of mind. Narrative procedures have been used in conjunction with false-belief tasks in prior studies and they have proved to be fruitful in eliciting a link between theory of mind and performance on a range of language measures (Capps *et al.*, 2000; Norbury and Bishop, 2003; Siller *et al.*, 2014). In the current study, false-belief tasks were not included as an insight into a narrator's theory of mind abilities could be elicited through references to frames of mind, including emotion terms, and the use of character speech during the narrative procedure. It may be useful, however, for future studies to include false-belief tasks to strengthen the association between interjectional usage, language abilities, and theory of mind. Also, the findings from this preliminary study provide a deeper insight into emotional expression through the use of interjections. Non-verbal aspects of emotion, such as facial expressions, have been the dominant focus in previous research to date whereas language used to express emotion warrants further investigation. Although non-verbal and verbal expressions are often treated as separate entities in prior research thus far, they can work in conjunction with one-another. Interjections are often accompanied by facial expressions and/or gestures; for example, *ouch* is an interjection used to express pain and this can be depicted upon a person's facial expression through lowering the eyebrows, tightening the eyelids, wrinkling the nose, and closing eyes (Prkachin, 1992). To date, no previous study has investigated the relationship between non-verbal expressions and interjections. This is another potential topic for further research to explore.

10.1 Limitations and Suggestions for Future Research

Although the current study yields interesting findings, there are some limitations which must be addressed. Firstly, the transcripts of the audio recordings during the narrative task and play sessions were coded by one person, the researcher. The context was known to the researcher as they worked with participants first-hand, which is significant as interjections are bound by context. An additional coder, however, would have contributed to the reliability of the findings. Secondly, the groups consisted of unequal and relatively small sample sizes. This should be taken into consideration when interpreting the results. Thus, it would be useful for future investigations to use a larger population sample which is evenly balanced. Asano's (1997, p. 4) study into interjectional usage, however, was based on transcripts of spoken discourse from twenty-eight children, aged between 11 months and 5 years 2 months, during parent-child interactions. Also, Stange's (2016, p. 76) study was based on transcripts of spoken discourse of twelve children aged between 1 year 8 months and 3 years old during play sessions. Thirty-six children participated in the current study, although groups were composed of uneven numbers of children and adolescents. For example, the ASD group consisted of one child and four adolescents whereas the TD group consisted of eight children. Future studies should aim to match participants according to age across all groups, taking these variables into account. Nevertheless, age was accounted for in the results through using CELF-5 standardised scores and multiple regression modelling. In the present study, groups were not matched according to biological sex which is another limitation. For example, 4 out of 5 participants with ASD were male, 9 out of 12 participants with ASD-LI were male, and 6 out of 11 participants with DLD were male. No typically developing male pupils participated in this study. Future research studies should aim to match participants according to biological sex as there is the possibility that it may elicit differences in interjectional usage. To date, previous studies of interjections have based their findings upon children's usage during play sessions. Thus, a fruitful topic for future research could include investigating the use of interjections in adolescence and adulthood as research into this has not yet been conducted. It is plausible to suggest that adolescents and adults produce more expletives than children. Expletives is another potential topic for further research considering that they can simultaneously function as interjections, as previously stated in chapter six. Finally, no typically developing adolescents participated in this study due to difficulties which arose during the recruitment process which is another limitation. Alongside the current study, I had obtained ethical approval from Newcastle University's Faculty of Medical Sciences Research Ethics Committee to conduct an additional study into the perception of speech sounds. Typically developing adults were recruited to take part in the study, and the format involved participants listening to a number of different cognitive, emotive, phatic, and volitive interjections which differ in valence and arousal. After listening to each interjection, participants are instructed to rate each sound and plot it on a dimensional space, similar to Figure 3. When doing so, participants would formulate an interpretation about the level of valence and arousal conveyed through the interjection uttered. However, the outbreak of COVID-19 and the restrictions which followed prohibited the additional study from being able to take place. Thus, examining the perception of interjections and their acoustic features may be a fruitful topic for future research.

Appendices

Appendix A: Ethical approval form from Newcastle University's Faculty of Medical Sciences.

Faculty of Medical Sciences

Newcastle University
The Medical School
Framlington Place
Newcastle upon Tyne
NE2 4HH United Kingdom

Sinead Corkett-Beirne
Institute of Neuroscience

FACULTY OF MEDICAL SCIENCES: ETHICS COMMITTEE

Dear Sinead,

Title: The use of interjections and cognitive state verbs by children diagnosed with Autism Spectrum Disorder, Developmental Language Disorder and Typically Developing children
Application No: 1491/4489/2018
Start date to end date: 14/05/2018 to 14/05/2019

On behalf of the Faculty of Medical Sciences Ethics Committee, I am writing to confirm that the ethical aspects of your proposal have been considered and your study has been given ethical approval.

The approval is limited to this project: **1491/4489/2018.** If you wish for a further approval to extend this project, please submit a re-application to the FMS Ethics Committee and this will be considered.

During the course of your research project you may find it necessary to revise your protocol. Substantial changes in methodology, or changes that impact on the interface between the researcher and the participants must be considered by the FMS Ethics Committee, prior to implementation.*

At the close of your research project, please report any adverse events that have occurred and the actions that were taken to the FMS Ethics Committee.*

Best wishes,

Yours sincerely

K. Sutherland.

Kimberley Sutherland
On behalf of Faculty Ethics Committee

cc.
Professor Daniel Nettle, Chair of FMS Ethics Committee
Mrs Kay Howes, Research Manager

*Please refer to the latest guidance available on the internal Newcastle web-site.

tel: +44 (0) 191 208 6000
fax: +44 (0) 191 208 6621

www.ncl.ac.uk
The University of Newcastle upon Tyne trading as Newcastle University

THE QUEEN'S
ANNIVERSARY PRIZES
FOR HIGHER AND FURTHER EDUCATION
2013

14/05/2018

The **Institute of Neuroscience**

The use of interjections by children and adolescents with Autism Spectrum Disorder, Developmental Language Disorder, and a typically developing cohort.

Information Sheet for Parents

Invitation

Your child is invited to take part in a research study. Before you decide if you want your child to get involved, it is important for you to understand why this study is being done and what it will involve. Please take your time to read the following information carefully and discuss it with others if you wish. Please ask if there is anything that is not clear or if you would like more information on what the study will involve. Thank you for reading this.

What is the purpose of the study?

The purpose of this study is to examine the use of certain language features in typically developing children in comparison to those of a similar age who have been diagnosed with Autism Spectrum Disorder and Developmental Language Disorder.

What is being tested?

I, the researcher, am looking at the use and recognition of interjections which are a feature of language used to express emotion. Examples include *wow, oops, uh oh* and *goodness gracious*. Interjections have not been studied before among typically developing individuals, nor have they been studied using individuals diagnosed with Autism Spectrum Disorder or Developmental Language Disorder. My research aims to bridge this gap.

Why has your child been chosen?

Your child has been asked to participate in this study as they match the following criteria: they are a native speaker of English and they are aged between five and sixteen years old. Typically developing children have been asked to take part alongside children who have been diagnosed with Autism Spectrum Disorder or Developmental Language Disorder. As each child is under the age of 18 years old parental consent is required.

Does my child have to take part?

No. It is up to you to decide whether or not you want your child to take part. If you decide that you want your child to join this study, you will be asked to sign a consent form to be returned. However, you will still be free to withdraw your child from the study at any time and without giving a reason. Children will be provided with a consent form to sign, however if they have difficulty with this then a parental signature will be required on this form as well. I will explain the project to each child prior to commencing research and emphasise that they do not have to take part if they do not wish to do so.

What will my child have to do?

Each child will be asked to complete two language assessments. After this, I will show them a wordless picture book and ask them to tell me a story using the book as a prompt. Your child will also play a game of snakes and ladders. I will record this using a Dictaphone so that I can analyse their spoken language later.

Will my taking part in the study be kept confidential?

All participants will remain anonymous and participation in the study will be kept strictly confidential. The participants will not be named in the project and they will not be addressed by their names during the recordings or when the files are stored on my own personal computer. I will assign a code to each child to ensure that they are not identified by their names therefore their participation will remain anonymous.

Where will the data be stored?

The data will be stored on a Dictaphone and my own personal computer that no one else has access to. If you agree, I will give your child's speech and language therapist a copy of the language assessments to help them with their therapy planning. The data will be deleted by wiping the Dictaphone of all recordings and pressing delete on the sound files stored on my own personal computer once my thesis has been submitted. I will also shred the record forms of the language assessments to ensure that this data has been destroyed once I have submitted my thesis and no longer require access to these.

What will happen with the results of the study?

I will conduct statistical analyses with the results from my study, and the findings will be used in my thesis. Upon completion, I will then submit this to Newcastle University's Institute of Neuroscience to obtain a Master of Philosophy degree. The data will be kept until May 2020 which is the date I am expected to have submitted my project. After submission, I will then delete the recordings from the Dictaphone and from my own personal computer.

Who is organising and funding the study?

The study will be self-funded by myself, the researcher.

Contact Details

The study contact details are listed below.

Thank you for taking time to read this information.

This study was approved by the Faculty of Medical Sciences Research Ethics Committee, part of Newcastle University's Research Ethics Committee. This committee contains members who are internal to the Faculty, as well as one external member. This study was reviewed by members of the committee, who must provide impartial advice and avoid significant conflicts of interests.

Institute of Neuroscience
Henry Wellcome Building
The Medical School
Framlington Place
Newcastle University
Newcastle upon Tyne, NE2 4HH

Study Contact: Miss Sinead Corkett-Beirne
Email: s.corkett-beirne@ncl.ac.uk

Appendix C: Parental consent form

14/05/2018

Parental Consent Form

8.	If applicable, I understand that speech and language therapists working for the Newcastle-upon-Tyne Hospitals NHS Foundation trust may request a copy of my child's language assessments to help them with therapy planning.	
	I agree that a copy of my child's language assessments can be given to speech and language therapists working for the Newcastle-upon-Tyne Hospitals NHS Foundation Trust if requested.	☐
	I do not want a copy of my child's language assessment to be given to speech and language therapists working for the Newcastle-upon-Tyne Hospitals NHS Foundation Trust.	☐
9.	I, the parent or guardian of the child taking part along with the researcher, agree to sign and date this informed consent form.	☐
10.	My child has consented to participate in this study as well, and has signed here to confirm this: _____ Date: _____ My child has agreed to participate in this study as they may not be competent to consent themselves (signed by parent or legal guardian): _____ Date: _____	

_____   _____   _____

Name of Parent or Guardian   Signature   Date

Project Title: The use of interjections by children and adolescents with Autism Spectrum Disorder, Developmental Language Disorder, and a typically developing cohort.
Main Contact: Miss Sinead Corkett-Beirne
Email: s.corkett-beirne@ncl.ac.uk

14/05/2018

The Institute of Neuroscience

Parental Consent Form

Researcher:

_____   _____   _____

Name of Researcher   Signature   Date

Project Title: The use of interjections by children and adolescents with Autism Spectrum Disorder, Developmental Language Disorder, and a typically developing cohort.
Main Contact: Miss Sinead Corkett-Beirne
Email: s.corkett-beirne@ncl.ac.uk

136

Appendix D: Child consent form

14/05/2018

Child Consent Form

I_____, confirm that (please tick box as appropriate):

1.	I understand that the researcher will show me a picture book. The researcher will read me a story. She will then ask me to read the story back.	☐
2.	I have been given the chance to ask questions.	☐
3.	I agree to take part.	☐
4.	I understand that I can stop taking part at any point. I do not have to say why. I won't be asked why I have stopped taking part.	☐
5.	I understand that I won't be named.	☐
6.	The use of the data has been explained to me.	☐
7.	I understand that the results may be shared with the Head teacher from the schools taking part. I agree to my results being shared. I do not want my results to be shared.	☐ ☐
8.	If applicable, I understand that speech and language therapists may want a copy of my assessments.	

Project Title: The use of interjections by children and adolescents with Autism Spectrum Disorder, Developmental Language Disorder, and s typically developing cohort.
Main Contact: Miss Sinead Corkett-Beirne
Email: s.corkett-beirne@ncl.ac.uk

137

Child Consent Form

	I agree that they can have a copy.	☐
	I do not want them to have a copy.	☐
9.	I, along with the researcher, agree to sign and date this form.	☐
10.	I have agreed to take part. I have signed below to confirm this: _____ Date: _____ My child has agreed to participate in this study as they may not be competent to consent themselves (signed by parent or legal guardian): _____ Date: _____	

_____   _____   _____

Name of Parent or Guardian   Signature   Date

Researcher:

_____   _____   _____

Name of Researcher   Signature   Date

Project Title: The use of interjections by children and adolescents with Autism Spectrum Disorder, Developmental Language Disorder, and s typically developing cohort.
Main Contact: Miss Sinead Corkett-Beirne
Email: s.corkett-beirne@ncl.ac.uk

138

References

Adolphs, R. (2001) 'The neurobiology of social cognition', *Current Opinion in Neurobiology*, 11(2), pp. 231-239.

Aijmer, K. (2002) *English Discourse Particles: Evidence from a corpus.* Amsterdam: John Benjamins Publishing Company.

Alarcón, M., Abrahams, B. S., Stone, J., Duvall, J. A., Perederiy, J. V., Bomar, J., Sebat, J., Wigler, M., Martin, C., Ledbetter, D., Nelson, S., Cantor, R. and Geschwind, D. (2008) 'Linkage, association, and gene-expression analyses identify CNTNAP2 as an autism-susceptibility gene', *The American Journal of Human Genetics*, 82(1), pp. 150-159.

Alborough, J (no date) *Creating Hug: The Inspiration for Hug.* Available at: http://jezalborough.com/bobo/creating-hug.html (Accessed: 06 July 2020)

Ameka, F. (1992) 'Interjections: the universal yet neglected part of speech', *Journal of Pragmatics*, 18(2-3), pp. 101-118.

Ameka, F. (1992) 'The meaning of phatic and conative interjections', *Journal of Pragmatics*, 18(2-3), pp. 245-271.

Ameka, F. (2006) *Interjections.* Available at: https://pure.mpg.de/rest/items/item_852625/component/file_852624/content (Accessed: 23 October 2018)

Ameka, F. K., and Wilkins, D. P. (2006) 'Interjections', in Östman, J. and Verschueren, J. (ed.) *Handbook of Pragmatics.* Amsterdam: John Benjamins Publishing Company, pp. 1-19.

American Psychiatric Association. (2000) *Diagnostic and Statistical Manual of Mental Disorders.* 4th edn. Washington: American Psychiatric Association.

American Psychiatric Association. (2013) *Diagnostic and Statistical Manual of Mental Disorders.* 5th edn. Arlington: American Psychiatric Association.

American Psychiatric Association. (2016) *DSM-5 update: supplement to diagnostic and statistical manual of mental disorders, fifth edition.* Available at: https://dsm.psychiatryonline.org/pb-assets/dsm/update/DSM5Update2016.pdf (Accessed: 20 August 2018)

Andrés-Roqueta, C., Adrian, J., Clemente, R. and Katsos, N. (2013) 'Which are the best predictors of theory of mind delay in children with specific language impairment?', *International Journal of Language and Communication Disorders*, 48(6), pp. 726-737.

Andrés-Roqueta, C. and Katsos, N. (2017) 'The contribution of grammar, vocabulary and theory of mind in pragmatic language competence in children with autistic spectrum disorders', *Frontiers in Psychology*, 8, pp. 1-5.

Asano, Y. (1997) 'Acquisition of English interjections ouch, yuck, and oops in early childhood', *Colorado Research in Linguistics*, 15, pp. 1-15.

Augustine, J. R. (2017) *Human Neuroanatomy.* 2nd edn. New Jersey: John Wiley & Sons, Inc.

Baars, B. J., and Gage, N. M. (2018) *Fundamentals of Cognitive Neuroscience: A Beginner's Guide.* 2nd edn. London: Academic Press.

Bailey, A., Le Couteur, A., Gottesman, I., Bolton, P., Simonoff, E., Yuzda, E. and Rutter, M. (1995) 'Autism as a strongly genetic disorder: evidence from a British twin study', *Psychological Medicine*, 25, pp. 63-77.

Baio, J., Wiggins, L., Christensen, D. L., Maenner, M. J., Daniels, J., Warren, Z., Kurzius-Spencer, M., Zahorodny, W., Robinson Rosenberg, C., White, T., Durkin, M. S., Imm, P., Nikolaou, L., Yeargin-Allsopp, M., Ching-Lee, L., Harrington, R., Lopez, M., Fitzgerald, R. T., Hewitt, A., Pettygrove, S., Constantino, J. N., Vehorn, A., Shenouda, J., Hall-Lande, J., Van Naarden Braun, K. and Dowling, N. F. (2018). *Prevalence of autism spectrum disorder among children aged 8 years – autism and developmental disabilities monitoring network, 11 sites, united states, 2014.* Available at: https://www.cdc.gov/mmwr/volumes/67/ss/ss6706a1.htm#suggestedcitation (Accessed: 11 March 2019)

Bamberg, M. and Damrad-Frye, R. (1991) 'On the ability to provide evaluative comments: further explorations of children's narrative competencies', *Journal of Child Language*, 18(3), pp. 689-710.

Banney, R. M., Harper-Hill, K. and Arnott, W. L. (2015) 'The Autism Diagnostic Observation Schedule and narrative assessment: Evidence for specific narrative impairments in autism spectrum disorders', *International Journal of Speech-Language Pathology*, 17(2), pp. 159-171.

Bänziger, T., Hosoya, G. and Scherer, K. (2015) 'Path Models of Vocal Emotion Communication', PLOS ONE, 10(9), pp. 1-29.

Baron-Cohen, S., Leslie, A. M. and Frith, U. (1985) 'Does the autistic child have a "theory of mind"?', *Cognition*, 21(1), pp. 37-46.

Baron-Cohen, S. (1995) *Mindblindness: An Essay on Autism and Theory of Mind*. United States of America: Massachusetts Institute of Technology.

Baron-Cohen, S. (2002) 'The extreme male brain theory of autism', *TRENDS in Cognitive Sciences*, 6(6), pp. 248-254.

Baron-Cohen, S., Lombardo, M., Aeuyeung, B., Ashwin, E., Chakrabarti, B. and Knickmeyer, R. (2011) 'Why are Autism Spectrum Conditions more prevalent in males?', *PLOS Biology*, 9(6), pp. 1-10.

Bartlett, C., Flax, J., Fermano, Z., Hare, A., Hou, L., Petrill, S., Buyske, S. and Brzustowicz, L. (2012) 'Gene x gene interaction in shared etiology of Autism and Specific Language Impairment', *Biological Psychiatry*, 72(8), pp. 692-699.

Bestelmeyer. P., Kotz, S. and Belin, P. (2017) 'Effects of emotional valence and arousal on the voice perception network', *Social Cognitive and Affective Neuroscience*, 12(8), pp. 1351-1358.

Bishop, D. V. M. (1989) 'Autism, Asperger's syndrome and Semantic-Pragmatic Disorder: Where are the boundaries?', *British Journal of Disorders of Communication*, 24(2), pp. 107-121.

Bishop, D. V. M. (2001) 'Genetic and environmental risks for specific language impairment in children', *Philosophical Transactions of the Royal Society. Series B: Biological Sciences*, 356(1407), pp. 369-380.

Bishop, D. V. M. (2006) 'What causes specific language impairment in children?', *Current Directions in Psychological Science*, 15(5), pp. 217-221.

Bishop, D. V. M. (2009) 'Genes, cognition, and communication', *Annals of the New York Academy of Sciences*, 1156(1), pp. 1-18.

Bishop, D. V. M. (2010) 'Overlaps between Autism and Language Impairment: Phenomimicry or shared etiology?', *Behavior Genetics*, 40(5), pp. 618-629.

Bishop, D. V. M. and Edmundson, A. (1987) 'Language-impaired 4-year-olds: distinguishing transient from persistent impairment', *Journal of Speech and Hearing Disorders*, 52(2), pp. 156-173.

Bishop, D. V. M., Snowling, M., Thompson, P. and Greenhalgh, T. (2017) 'Phase 2 of catalise: a multinational and multidisciplinary delphi consensus study of problems with language development: terminology', *The Journal of Child Psychology and Psychiatry*, 58(10), pp. 1068-1080.

Blom, E. and Boerma, T. (2016) 'Why do children with language impairment have difficulties with narrative macrostructure?', *Research in Developmental Disabilities*, 55, pp. 301-311.

Bolinger, D. (1989) *Intonation and Its Uses: Melody in Grammar and Discourse.* London: Edward Arnold.

Borchmann, S. (2019) 'Non-spontaneous and communicative emotive interjections', *Scandinavian Studies in Language*, 10(1), pp. 7-40.

Botting, N. (2002) 'Narrative as a tool for the assessment of linguistic and pragmatic impairments', *Child Language Teaching and Therapy*, 18(1), pp. 1-21.

Brazis, P. W., Masdeu, J. C. and Biller, J. (2011) *Localization in Clinical Neurology.* 6th edn. Philadelphia: Lippincott Williams & Wilkins.

Brinton, B., Fujiki, M. and Asai, N. (2019) 'The ability of five children with Developmental Language Disorder to describe mental states in stories', *Communication Disorders Quarterly*, 40(2), pp. 109-116.

Brodal, P. (2004) *The Central Nervous System: Structure and Function.* 3rd edn. New York: Oxford University Press.

Brownell, R. (2000) *Expressive One-Word Picture Vocabulary Test: Manual.* 4th edn. California: Academic Therapy Publications.

Brugha, T., Cooper, S. A., McManus, S., Purdon, S., Smith, J., Scott, F. J., Spiers, N. and Tyrer, F. (2012) *Estimating the prevalence of autism spectrum conditions in adults: Extending the 2007 adult psychiatric morbidity survey.* Available at: http://www.wecommunities.org/MyNurChat/archive/LDdownloads/Est_Prev_Autism_S pec_Cond_in_Adults_Report.pdf (Accessed: 14 May 2021)

Buchanan, T., Lutz, K., Mirzazade, S., Specht, K., Shah, N., Zilles, K. and Jäncke, L. (2000) 'Recognition of emotional prosody and verbal components of spoken language: an fMRI study', *Cognitive Brain Research*, 9(3), pp. 227-238.

Capps, L., Losh. M. and Thurber, C. (2000) '"The Frog Ate the Bug and Made his Mouth Sad": Narrative Competence in Children with Autism', *Journal of Abnormal Child Psychology*, 2, pp. 193-204.

Castelli, F. (2005) 'Understanding emotions from standardized facial expressions in autism and normal development', *Autism* 9(4), pp. 428-449.

Charman, T., Pickles, A., Simonoff, E., Chandler, S., Loucas, T. and Baird, G. (2011) 'IQ in children with autism spectrum disorders: data from the special needs and autism project (SNAP)', *Psychological Medicine*, 41(3), pp. 619-627.

Cherry, K. (2020) *Functions of the somatic nervous system*. Available at: https://www.verywellmind.com/what-is-the-somatic-nervous-system-2795866 (Accessed: 24 April 2020)

Chismar, D. (1988) 'Empathy and sympathy: the important difference', *The Journal of Value Inquiry*, 22(4), pp. 257-266.

Chomsky, N. (2002) *On Nature and Language*. Cambridge: Cambridge University Press.

Chomsky, N. (2006) *Language and Mind*. 3rd ed. Cambridge: Cambridge University Press.

Chomsky, N. and Halle, M. (1968) *The Sound Pattern of English*. New York: Harper and Row.

Clark, D. L., Boutros, N. N. and Mendez, M. F. (2018) *The Brain and Behaviour: An Introduction to Behavioral Neuroanatomy*. 4th edn. Cambridge: Cambridge University Press.

Clark, H. H. and Fox Tree, J. E. (2002) 'Using uh and um in spontaneous speaking', *Cognition*, 84(1), pp. 73-111.

Colozzo, P., Gillam, R. B., Wood, M., Schnell, R. D. and Johnston, J. R. (2011) 'Content and form in the narratives of children with specific language impairment', *Journal of Speech, Language, and Hearing Research*, 54(6), pp. 1609-1627.

Crane, L., Chester, J., Goddard, L., Henry, L. and Hill, E. (2016) 'Experiences of autism diagnosis: a survey of over 1000 parents in the United Kingdom', *Autism*, 20(2), pp. 153-162.

Cross, M. (2011) *Children with social, emotional and behavioural difficulties and communication problems: There is always a reason*. 2nd edn. London: Jessica Kingsley Publishers.

Cruse, A. (2004) *Meaning in Language: An Introduction to Semantics and Pragmatics.* 2nd edn. Oxford: Oxford University Press.

Darwin, C. (1872) *The Expression of the Emotions in Man and Animals.* New York: Cambridge University Press.

Davenport, M., and Hannahs, S. J. (2010) *Introducing Phonetics and Phonology.* 3rd edn. Oxon: Routledge.

De Fossé, L., Hodge, S. M., Makris, N., Kennedy, D. N., Caviness Jr, V. S., McGrath, L., Steele, S., Ziegler, D. A., Herbert, M. R, Frazier, J. A., Tager-Flusberg, H. and Harris, G. J. (2004) 'Language-association cortex asymmetry in autism and specific language impairment', *Annals of Neurology*, 56(6), pp. 757-766.

Devlin, H (no date) *Introduction to FMRI.* Available at: https://www.ndcn.ox.ac.uk/divisions/fmrib/what-is-fmri/introduction-to-fmri (Accessed: 25 July 2020)

Dietrich, S., Hertrich, I., Alter, K., Ischebeck, A. and Ackermann, H. (2008) 'Understanding the emotional expression of verbal interjections: a functional MRI study', *Brain Imaging*, 19(18), pp. 1751-1755.

Downing, A. and Martínez Caro, E. (2019) 'Interjections and emotions: The case of gosh', in Lachlan Mackenzie, J. and Alba-Juez, L. (ed.) *Emotion in Discourse.* Amsterdam: John Benjamins Publishing Company, pp. 87-112.

Duinmeijer, I., de Jong, J. and Scheper, A. (2012) 'Narrative abilities, memory and attention in children with a specific language impairment', *International Journal of Language and Communication Disorders*, 47(5), pp. 542-555.

Dunn, L. M. and Dunn, M. D. (2007) *Peabody Picture Vocabulary Test.* 4th edn. Texas: NCS Pearson Inc.

Dunn, L. M., Dunn, M. D., Sewell, J., Styles, B., Brzyska, B., Shamsan, Y. and Burge, B. (2009) *The British Picture Vocabulary Scale.* 3rd edn. London: GL Assessment Limited.

Ekman, P. (1979) 'About brows: emotional and conversational signals', in von Cranach, M., Foppa, K., Lepenies, W. and Ploog, D. (ed.) *Human Ethology.* Cambridge: Cambridge University Press.

Ekman, P. (1992) 'An argument for basic emotions', *Cognition and Emotion*, 6(3-4), pp. 169-200.

Ekman, P (no date) *Fear*. Available at: https://www.paulekman.com/universal-emotions/what-is-fear/ (Accessed: 08 May 2021)

Ekman, P (no date) *What is disgust?* Available at: https://www.paulekman.com/universal-emotions/what-is-disgust/ (Accessed: 26 July 2020)

Ekman, P. and Cordaro, D. (2011) 'What is meant by calling emotions basic', *Emotion Review*, 3(4), pp. 364-370.

Ekman, P. and Friesen, W. V. (2003) *Unmasking the Face: A Guide to Recognizing Emotions from Facial Clues*. California: Malor Books.

Elder, J., Kreider, C., Brasher, S. and Ansell, M. (2017) 'Clinical impact of early diagnosis of autism on the prognosis and parent-child relations', *Psychology Research and Behavior Management*, 10, pp. 283-292.

Engberg-Pedersen, E. and Vang Christensen, R. (2017) 'Mental states and activities in Danish narratives: children with autism and children with language impairment*', *Journal of Child Language*, 44(5), pp. 1192-1217.

Engel de Abreu, P. M. J., Conway, A. R. A., and Gathercole, S. E. (2010) 'Working memory and fluid intelligence in young children', *Intelligence*, 38(6), pp. 552-561.

Farrar, M. J., Johnson, B., Tompkins, V., Easters, M., Zilisi-Medus, A. and Benigno, J. P. (2009) 'Language and theory of mind in preschool children with specific language impairment', *Journal of Communication Disorders*, 42(6), pp. 428-441.

Farrar, M. J., Kyeung Seung, H. and Lee, H. (2017) 'Language and false-belief task performance in children with autism spectrum disorder', *Journal of Speech, Language, and Hearing Research*, 60(7), pp. 1999-2013.

Fein, D., Barton, M., Eigsti, I., Kelley, E., Naigles, L., Schultz, R. T., Stevens, M., Helt, M., Orinstein, A., Rosenthal, M., Troyb, E. and Tyson, K. (2013) 'Optimal outcome in individuals with a history of autism', *Journal of Child Psychology and Psychiatry*, 54(2), pp. 195-205.

Fenson, L., Dale, P. S., Reznick, J. S., Bates, E., Thal, D. J., Pethick, S. J., Tomasello, M., Mervis, C. B. and Stiles, J. (1994) 'Variability in early communicative development', *Monographs of the Society for Research in Child Development*, 59(5), pp. 1-185.

Folstein, S. and M. Rutter. (1977) 'Genetic influences and infantile autism', *Nature*, 265, pp. 726-728.

Ford, J. A. and Milosky, L. M. (2003) 'Inferring emotional reactions in social situations: differences in children with language impairment', *Journal of Speech, Language, and Hearing Research*, 46(1), pp. 21-30.

Fraser, B. (1990) 'An approach to discourse markers', *Journal of Pragmatics*, 14(3), pp. 383-395.

Frith, U. and Happé, F. (1994) 'Autism: beyond "theory of mind"', *Cognition*, 50(1-3), pp. 115-132.

Fujiki, M., Spackman, M. P., Brinton, B. and Illig, T. (2008) 'Ability of children with language impairment to understand emotion conveyed by prosody in a narrative passage', *International Journal of Language and Communication Disorders*, 43(3), pp. 330-345.

Gauger, L., Lombardino, L. and Leonard, C. (1997) 'Brain morphology in children with specific language impairment', *Journal of Speech, Language, and Hearing Research*, 40(6), pp. 1272-1284.

Gazzaniga, M., Ivry, R. and Mangan, G. (2009) *Cognitive Neuroscience: The Biology of the Mind.* 3rd edn. London: W. W. Norton & Company.

German, D. J. (2000) *Test of Word Finding.* 2nd edn. Texas: Pearson.

Gillott, A., Furniss, F. and Walter, A. (2004) 'Theory of mind ability in children with specific language impairment', *Child Language Teaching and Therapy*, 20(1), pp. 1-11.

Gleason, J. (2005) *The Development of Language.* United States of America: Pearson Education, Inc.

Goddard, C. (2014) 'Interjections and emotion (with special reference to "surprise" and "disgust")', *Emotion Review*, 6(1), pp. 53-63.

Godfrey, H. K. and Grimshaw, G. M. (2016) 'Emotional language is all right: emotional prosody reduces hemispheric asymmetry for linguistic processing', *Laterality: Asymmetries of Body, Brain and Cognition*, 21(4-6), pp. 568-584.

Goffman, E. (1978) 'Response cries', *Language*, 54(4), pp. 787-815.

Gorman, K., Olson, L., Presmanes Hill, A., Lunsford, R., Heeman, P. A. and van Santen, J. P. H. (2016) 'Uh and um in children with autism spectrum disorders or language impairment', *Autism Research*, 9(8), pp. 854-865.

Grazzani, I., Ornaghi, V., Conte, E., Pepe, A. and Caprin, C. (2018) 'The relation between emotion understanding and theory of mind in children aged 3 to 8: the key role of language', *Frontiers in Psychology*, 9, pp. 1-10.

Grossman, R. B., Edelson, L. R. and Tager-Flusberg, H. (2013) 'Emotional facial and vocal Expressions during story retelling and adolescents with high-functioning autism', *Journal of Speech, Language and Hearing Research*, 56(3), pp. 1035-1044.

Hagoort, P. (2005) 'On Broca, brain, and binding: a new framework', *Trends in Cognitive Sciences*, 9(9), pp. 416-423.

Halladay, A., Bishop, S., Constantino, J., Daniels, A., Koenig, K., Palmer, K., Messinger, D., Pelphrey, K., Sanders, S., Tepper Singer, A., Lounds Taylor, J. and Szatmari, P. (2015) 'Sex and gender differences in autism spectrum disorder: summarizing the evidence gaps and identifying emerging areas of priority', *Molecular Autism*, 6(1), pp. 1-5.

Happé, F. (1994) *Autism: an introduction to psychological theory*. London: UCL Press Limited.

Happé, F. (1995) 'The role of age and verbal ability in the theory of mind task performance of subjects with autism', *Child Development*, 66(3), pp. 843-855.

Heaton, P., Reichenbacher, L., Sauter, D., Allen, R., Scott, S. and Hill, E. (2012) 'Measuring the effects of alexithymia on perception of emotional vocalizations in autism spectrum disorder and typical development', *Psychological Medicine*, 42(11), pp. 2453-2459.

Hepach, R., Kliemann, D., Grünelsen, S., Heekeren, H. R. and Dziobek, I. (2011) 'Conceptualizing emotions along the dimensions of valence, arousal, and communicative frequency – implications for social-cognitive tests and training tools', *Frontiers in Psychology*, 2, pp. 1-6.

Hobson, R. P. and Lee, A. (1989) 'Emotion-related and abstract concepts in autistic people: evidence from the British Picture Vocabulary Scale', *Journal of Autism and Developmental Disorders*, 19(4), pp. 601-623.

Howlin, P. and Asgharian, A. (1999) 'The diagnosis of autism and Asperger syndrome: findings from a survey of 770 families', *Developmental Medicine & Child Neurology*, 41(12), pp. 834-839.

Ibanez, A., Huepe, D., Gempp, R., Gutiérrez, V., Rivera-Rei, A. and Toledo, M. I. (2013) 'Empathy, sex and fluid intelligence as predictors of theory of mind', *Personality and Individual Differences*, 54(5), pp. 616-621.

Irshad, M. (2018) *The Cerebrum*. Available at:
https://teachmeanatomy.info/neuroanatomy/structures/cerebrum/ (Accessed: 19 May 2021)

Irvine, C. A., Eigsti, I. and Fein, D. A. (2016) 'Uh, um, and autism: filler disfluencies as pragmatic markers in adolescents with optimal outcomes from autism spectrum disorder', *Journal of Autism and Developmental Disorders*, 46(3), pp. 1061-1070.

Just, M. A., Keller, T. A., Malave, V. L., Kana, R. K. and Varma, S. (2012) 'Autism as a neural systems disorder: a theory of frontal-posterior underconnectivity', *Neuroscience and Biobehavioral Reviews*, 36(4), pp. 1292-1313.

Justice, L. M., Bowles, R., Pence, K. and Gosse, C. (2010) 'A scalable tool for assessing children's language abilities within a narrative context: The NAP (Narrative Assessment Protocol)', *Early Childhood Research Quarterly*, 25(2), pp. 218-234.

Kaderavek, J. N., and Sulzby, E. (2000) 'Narrative production by children with and without specific language impairment: oral narratives and emergent readings', *Journal of Speech, Language, and Hearing Research*, 43(1), pp. 34-49.

Kirk, S. A., McCarthy, J. D. and Kirk, W. S. (1968) *Illinois Test of Psycholinguistic Abilities (ITPA)*. Illinois: University of Illinois Press.

Kjelgaard, M. M. and Tager-Flusberg, H. (2001) 'An investigation of language impairment in autism: implications for genetic subgroups', *Language and Cognitive Processes*, 16(2-3), pp. 287-308.

Kjellmer, L., Hedvall, A., Holm, A., Fernell, E., Gillberg, C. and Norrelgen, F. (2012) 'Language comprehension in pre-schoolers with autism spectrum disorders without intellectual disability: use of the reynell developmental language scales', *Research in Autism Spectrum Disorders*, 6(3), pp. 1119-1125.

Korkman, M., Kirk, U. and Kemp, S. L. (2008) *NEPSY-II: Lasten neuropsykologinen tutkimus (NEPSY: II: Children's neuropsychological investigation)*. Helsinki: Psykologien Kustannus Oy.

Kotz, S. A. and Paulmann, S. (2011) 'Emotion, language, and the brain', *Language and Linguistics Compass*, 5(3), pp. 108-125.

Kover, S., Haebig, E., Oakes, A., McDuffie, A., Hagerman, R. and Abbeduto, L. (2014) 'Sentence comprehension in boys with autism spectrum disorder', *American Journal of Speech-Language Pathology*, 23(3), pp. 385-394.

Kulusza Jr. R. J., Lukose, R. and Veith Stevens, L. (2011) 'Malformation of the human superior olive in autistic spectrum disorders', *Brain Research*, 1367, pp. 360-371.

Lartseva, A., Dijkstra, T. and Buitelaar, J. K. (2015) 'Emotional language processing in autism spectrum disorders: a systematic review', *Frontiers in Human Neuroscience*, 8, pp. 1-24.

Leonard, L. (2014) *Children with Specific Language Impairment.* 2nd ed. USA: Massachusetts Institute of Technology.

Lind, S. E. and Bowler, D. M. (2009) 'Language and theory of mind in autism spectrum disorder: the relationship between complement syntax and false belief task performance', *Journal of Autism and Developmental Disorders*, 39(6), pp. 929-937.

Lord, C., Elsabbagh, M., Baird, G. and Veenstra-Vandeeweele, J. (2018) 'Autism spectrum disorder', *Lancet*, 392, pp. 508-20.

Lord, C., Risi, S., Lambrecht, L., Cook Jr, E. H., Leventhal, B. L., DiLavore, P. C., Pickles, A. and Rutter, M. (2000) 'The autism diagnostic observation schedule – generic: a standard measure of social and communication deficits associated with the spectrum of autism', *Journal of Autism and Developmental Disorders*, 30(3), pp.205-223.

Losh, M. and Capps, L. (2003) 'Narrative ability in high-functioning children with Autism or Asperger's Syndrome*', *Journal of Autism and Developmental Disorders*, 33(3), pp. 239-251.

Lukose, R., Schmidt, E., Wolski Jr, T. P., Murawski, N. J. and Kulesza Jr, R. J. (2011) 'Malformation of the superior olivary complex in an animal model of autism', *Brain Research*, 1398, pp. 102-112.

Lukose, R., Beebe, K. and Kulesza Jr, R. J. (2015) 'Organisation of the human superior olivary complex in 15q duplication syndromes and autism spectrum disorders', *Neuroscience*, 286, pp. 216-230.

Lyons, J. (1981) *Language, Meaning and Context.* Suffolk, United Kingdom: The Chaucer Press.

MacKay, G. and Shaw, A. (2004) 'A comparative study of figurative language in children with autistic spectrum disorders', *Child Language Teaching and Therapy*, 20(1), pp. 13-32.

Manolitsi, M. and Botting, N. (2011) 'Language abilities in children with autism and language impairment: using narrative as a additional source of clinical information', *Child Language Teaching and Therapy*, 27(1), pp. 39-55.

Meng, K. and Schrabback, S. (1999) 'Interjections in adult-child discourse: The cases of German HM and NA', *Journal of Pragmatics*, 31(10), pp. 1263-1287.

Maynard, A. S., Monk, J. D. and Wilson Booker, K. (2011) 'Building empathy through identification and expression of emotions: a review of interactive tools for children with social deficits', *Journal of Creativity in Mental Health*, 6(2), pp. 166-175.

MacWhinney, B. (2000) *The CHILDES Project: Tools for Analysing Talk.* 3rd edn. Mahwah, NJ: Lawrence Erlbaum Associates.

McGregor, K. K. (2020) 'How we fail children with Developmental Language Disorder', *Language, Speech, and Hearing Services in Schools*, 51(4), pp. 981-992.

Merkenschlager, A., Amorosa, H., Kiefl, H. and Martinius, J. (2012) 'Recognition of face identity and emotion in expressive specific language impairment', *Folia Phoniatrica et Logopaedica*, 64(2), pp. 73-79.

Metcalfe, C., M. Grube, D. Gabriel, S. Dietrich, H. Ackermann, V. Cook and K. Alter. 2009. 'The processing of emotional utterances: contributions of prosodic and lexical information' in Alter, K., Horne, M., Lindgren, M., Roll, M. and von Koss Torkildsen, J. (ed.) *Braintalk: Discourse with and in the brain.* Lund: Media-Tryck.

Mey, J. L. (2001) *Pragmatics: an introduction.* 2nd edn. Oxford: Blackwell Publishers Ltd.

Mitchell, R. L. C. and Phillips, L. H. (2015) 'The overlapping relationship between emotion perception and theory of mind', *Neuropsychologia*, 70, pp. 1-10.

Mody, M. and Belliveau, J. W. (2013) 'Speech and language impairments in autism: insights from behavior and neuroimaging', *North American Journal of Medical Sciences*, 5(3), pp. 157-161.

Møller, A. R. (2006) *Hearing: Anatomy, Physiology, and Disorders of the Auditory System.* 2nd edn. United States of America: Elsevier.

Murray Sherman, S. and Guillery, R. W. (2002) 'The role of the thalamus in the flow of information to the cortex', *Philosophical Transactions: Biological Sciences*, 357(1428), pp. 1695-1708.

National Autistic Society (2018) *Social stories and comic strip conversations.* Available at: https://www.autism.org.uk/about/strategies/social-stories-comic-strips.aspx (Accessed: 05 August 2019)

National Health Service (2019) *Functional magnetic resonance imaging (fMRI).* Available at: https://www.gosh.nhs.uk/conditions-and-treatments/procedures-and-treatments/functional-magnetic-resonance-imaging-fmri (Accessed: 25 July 2020)

National Health Service (2016) *Overview: autism spectrum disorder (ASD).* Available at: https://www.nhs.uk/conditions/autism/ (Accessed: 20 August 2018)

National Health Service (no date) *Speech and language development from birth to 12 months.* Available at: https://www.gosh.nhs.uk/medical-information-0/procedures-and-treatments/speech-and-language-development-birth-12-months (Accessed: 15 May 2020)

National Institutes of Health (2018) *What are the parts of the nervous system?* Available at: https://www.nichd.nih.gov/health/topics/neuro/conditioninfo/parts (Accessed: 24 April 2020)

National Institutes of Health (2019) *Williams syndrome.* Available at: https://ghr.nlm.nih.gov/condition/williams-syndrome#resources (Accessed: 03 September 2019)

Noback, C. R., Strominger, N. L., Demarest, R. J. and Ruggiero, D. A. (2005) *The Human Nervous System: Structure and Function.* 6th edn. United States of America: Humana Press Inc.

Norbury, C. F. (2011) 'Developmental Language Disorders: Overview', in Howlin, P. A., Charman, R. and Ghaziuddin, M. (ed.) *The SAGE Handbook of Developmental Disorders.* Oxford: SAGE Publications Ltd.

Norbury, C. F. and Bishop, D. V. M. (2003) 'Narrative skills of children with communication impairments', *International Journal of Language and Communication Disorders*, 38(3), pp. 287-313.

Norbury, C. F., Gemmell, T. and Paul, R. (2014) 'Pragmatic abilities in narrative production: a cross-disorder comparison*', *Journal of Child Language*, 41(3), pp. 485-510.

Norbury, C. F., Gooch, D., Wray, C., Baird, G., Charman, T., Simonoff, E., Vamvakas, G. and Pickles, A. (2016) 'The impact of nonverbal ability on prevalence and clinical presentation of language disorder: evidence from a population study', *The Journal of Child Psychology and Psychiatry*, 57(11), pp. 1247-1257.

Norrick, N. (2009) 'Interjections as pragmatic markers', *Journal of Pragmatics*, 41(5), pp. 866-891.

O' Connell, D. C. and Kowal, S. (2005) 'Uh and um revisited: are they interjections for signaling delay?', *Journal of Psycholinguistic Research*, 34(6), pp. 555-576.

O'Neil, J. N., Connelly, C. J., Limb, C. J. and Ryugo, D. K. (2011) 'Syntactic morphology and the influence of auditory experience', *Hearing Research,* 279(1-2), pp. 118-130.

Pang E. W., Valica, T., MacDonald, M. J., Taylor, M. J., Brian, J., Lerch, J. P. and Anagnostou, E. (2016) 'Abnormal brain dynamics underlie speech production in children with autism spectrum disorder', *Autism Research*, 9(2), pp. 249-261.

Parikh, P. (2000) 'Communication, Meaning, and Interpretation', *Linguistics and Philosophy*, 23(2), pp. 185-212.

Peterson, D. C., Reddy, V. and Hamel, R. N. (2020) *Neuroanatomy, Auditory Pathway*. Available at: https://www.ncbi.nlm.nih.gov/books/NBK532311/ (Accessed: 02 May 2020)

Pexman, P. M., Rostad, K. R., McMorris, C. A., Climie, E. A., Stowkowy, J. and Glenwright. M. R. (2011) 'Processing of ironic language in children with high-functioning Autism Spectrum Disorder', *Journal of Autism and Developmental Disorders*, 41(8), pp. 1097-1112.

Pickles, A., St. Clair, M. C. and Conti-Ramsden, G. (2013) 'Communication and social deficits in relatives of individuals with SLI and relatives of individuals with ASD', *Journal of Autism and Developmental Disorders*, 43, pp. 156-167.

Pons, F., Lawson, J., Harris, P. L. and de Rosnay, M. (2003) 'Individual differences in children's emotion understanding: effects of age and language', *Scandinavian Journal of Psychology*, 44(4), pp. 347-353.

Poquérusse, J., Pastore, L., Dellantonio, S. and Esposito, G. (2018) 'Alexithymia and Autism Spectrum Disorder: A Complex Relationship', *Frontiers in Psychology*, 9, pp. 1196-1205.

Prkachin, K. M. (1992) 'The consistency of facial expressions of pain: a comparison across modalities', *Pain,* 51(3), pp. 297-306.

Preckel, K., Kanske, P. and Singer, T. (2018) 'On the interaction of social affect and cognition: empathy, compassion and theory of mind', *Current Opinion in Behavioural Sciences*, 19, pp. 1-6.

Premack, D. and Woodruff, G. (1978) 'Does the chimpanzee have a theory of mind?', *The Behavioural and Brain Sciences*, 4(1), pp. 515-526.

Prizant, B. M., and Rydell, P. J. (1984) 'Analysis of functions of delayed echolalia in autistic children', *Journal of Speech, Language, and Hearing Research*, 27(2), pp. 183-192.

Pulkki, V. and Karjalainen, M. (2015) *Communication Acoustics: An introduction to speech, audio and psychoacoustics*. Sussex: John Wiley & Sons, Ltd.

Pyers, J. E. and Senghas, A. (2009) 'Language promotes false-belief understanding', *Psychological Science*, 20(7), pp. 805-812.

Rapin, I. (1996) 'Practitioner review: developmental language disorders: a clinical update', *Journal of Child Psychology and Psychiatry*, 37(6), pp. 643-655.

Reber, A. S., Allen, R. and Reber, E. S. (2009) *The Penguin Dictionary of Psychology.* 4th edn. London: Penguin Books Ltd.

Reilly, J., Klima, E. S. and Bellugi, U. (1990) 'Once more with feeling: Affect and language in atypical populations', *Development and Psychopathology*, 2(4), pp. 367-391.

Reilly, J., Losh, M., Bellugi, U. and Wulfeck, B. (2004) '"Frog, where are you?" Narratives in children with specific language impairment, early focal brain injury, and Williams syndrome'. *Brain and Language*, 88(2), pp. 229-247.

Ricciardi, L., Demartini, B., Fotopoulou, A. and Edwards, M. J. (2015) 'Alexithymia in Neurological Disease: A Review', *The Journal of Neuropsychiatry and Clinical Neurosciences*, 27(3), pp. 179-187.

Richardson, M. (2006) *The respiratory system – Part 1: nose, pharynx and larynx*. Available at: https://www.nursingtimes.net/clinical-archive/respiratory-clinical-archive/the-respiratory-system-part-1-nose-pharynx-and-larynx-23-05-2006/ (Accessed: 13 August 2020)

Roberts, J. (2014) 'Echolalia and language development in children with autism', in Arciuli, J. and Brock, J. (ed.) *Communication in Autism*. Amsterdam: John Benjamins Publishing Company, pp. 53-74.

Rosset, E., and Rottman, J. (2014) 'The big 'whoops!' in the study of intentional behaviour: an appeal for a new framework in understanding human actions', *Journal of Cognition and Cognition*, 14(1-2), pp. 27-39.

Royal College of Speech and Language Therapists. (2017) *RCSLT briefing paper on Language Disorder with a specific focus on Developmental Language Disorder.* Available at: https://www.rcslt.org/wp-content/uploads/media/Project/RCSLT/language-disorder-briefing-paper.pdf (Accessed: 26 August 2021)

Russell, J. A. (1980) 'A circumplex model of affect', *Journal of Personality and Social Psychology*, 39(6), pp. 1161-1178.

Salzman, C. D. and Fusi, S. (2010) 'Emotion, cognition, and mental state representation in amygdala and prefrontal cortex', *Annual Review of Neuroscience*, 33(1), pp. 173-202.

Scherer, K. (1987) *Toward a dynamic theory of emotion: the component process model of affective states.* Available at: https://pdfs.semanticscholar.org/4c23/c3099b3926d4b02819f2af196a86d2ef16a1.pdf?_ga=2.166258878.128584654.1571749486-1491499791.1571749486 (Accessed: 13 August 2020)

Scherer, K. (2005) 'What are emotions? And how can they be measured?', *Social Science Information*, 44(4), pp. 693-727.

Scherer, K. R. and Juslin, P. N. (2008) 'Vocal expression of affect', in Harrigan, J., Rosenthal, R. and Scherer, K. R. (ed.) *The New Handbook of Methods in Nonverbal Behavior Research.* United States: Oxford University Press.

Semel, E., Wiig, E. H. and Secord, W. (1987) *Clinical Evaluation of Language Fundamentals – Revised.* San Antonio, TX: The Psychological Corporation.

Serafini, F. (2014) 'Exploring wordless picture books', *The Reading Teacher*, 68(1), pp. 24-26.

Schirmer, A. and Kotz, S. A. (2006) 'Beyond the right hemisphere: brain mechanisms mediating vocal emotional processing', *TRENDS in Cognitive Sciences,* 10(1), pp. 24-30.

Shattuck, P., Mailick Seltzer, M., Greenberg, J., Orsmond, G., Bolt, D., Kring, S., Lounds, J. and Lord, C. (2007) 'Change in autism symptoms and maladaptive behaviors in adolescents and adults with autism spectrum disorder', *Journal of Autism and Developmental Disorders*, 37(9), pp. 1735-1747.

Siller, M., Swanson, M. R., Serlin, G. and George, A. (2014) 'Internal state language in the storybook narratives of children with and without autism spectrum disorder: investigating relations to theory of mind abilities', *Research in Autism Spectrum Disorders*, 8(5), pp. 589-596.

Spanoudis, G. (2016) 'Theory of mind and specific language impairment in school-age children', *Journal of Communication Disorders*, 61, pp. 83-96.

Sperber, D. and Wilson, D. (1986) *Relevance: Communication and Cognition.* Oxford: Basil Blackwell.

Sperber, D. and Wilson, D. (1995) *Relevance: Communication and Cognition.* 2nd edn. Oxford: Blackwell Publishing.

Sperber, D. and Wilson, D. (2002) 'Pragmatics, modularity and mind-reading', *Mind & Language*, 17(1-2), pp. 3-23.

Stange, U. (2016) *Emotive Interjections in British English: A corpus-based study on variation in acquisition, function and usage.* Amsterdam: John Benjamins Publishing Company.

St Clair, M., Pickles, A., Durkin, K. and Conti-Ramsden, G. (2011) 'A longitudinal study of behavioural, emotional and social difficulties in individuals with a history of specific language impairment (sli)', *Journal of Communication Disorders*, 44(2), pp. 186-199.

Stein, N. L., and Glenn, C. G. (1975) *An analysis of story comprehension in elementary school children.* Available at: https://files.eric.ed.gov/fulltext/ED121474.pdf (Accessed: 13 August 2020)

Stromswold, K. (1998) 'Genetics of spoken language disorders', *Human Biology*, 70, pp. 297-324.

Surian, L., Baron-Cohen, S. and Van der Lely, H. (1996) 'Are children with autism deaf to Gricean maxims?', *Cognitive Neuropsychiatry*, 1(1), pp. 55-71.

Sutton, M. (2017) *Child Language: Acquisition and Development.* 2nd edn. London: SAGE Publications.

Scherer, K. R. (1986) 'Vocal Affect Expression: A Review and a Model for Future Research', *Psychological Bulletin*, 99(2), pp. 143-165.

Szameitat, D. P., Alter, K., Szameitat, A. J., Darwin, C. J., Wildgruber, D., Dietrich, S. and Sterr, A. (2009) 'Differentiation of emotions in laughter at the behavioral level', *Emotion*, 9(3), pp. 397-405.

Tager-Flusberg, H. and Sullivan, K. (1995) 'Attributing mental states to story characters: a comparison of narratives produced by autistic and mentally retarded individuals', *Applied Psycholinguistics*, 16(3), pp. 241-256.

Tager-Flusberg, H. and Joseph, R. M. (2003) 'Identifying neurocognitive phenotypes in autism', *Philosophical Transactions: Biological Sciences*, 358(1430), pp. 303-314.

Tager-Flusberg, H (2011) *False-belief tasks are distinct from theory of mind.* Available at: https://www.spectrumnews.org/opinion/viewpoint/false-belief-tasks-are-distinct-from-theory-of-mind/ (Accessed: 05 August 2019)

Tager-Flusberg, H. (2015) 'Defining language impairments in a subgroup of children with autism spectrum disorder', *Science China Life Sciences*, 58(10), pp. 1044-1052.

Taylor, G. J., Bagby, R. M. and Parker, J. D. A. (1991) 'The Alexithymia Construct: A Potential Paradigm for Psychosomatic Medicine', *Psychomatics*, 32(2), pp. 153-164.

Taylor, L. J., Mayberry, M. T., Grayndler, L. and Whitehouse, A. J. O. (2015) 'Evidence for shared deficits in identifying emotions from faces and from voices in autism spectrum disorders and specific language impairment', *International Journal of Language and Communication Disorders*, 50(4), pp. 452-466.

Teh, E. J., Yap, M. J. and Rickard Liow, S. J. (2018) 'Emotional processing in autism spectrum disorders: effects of age, emotional valence, and social engagement on emotional language use', *Journal of Autism and Developmental Disorders*, 48(12), pp. 4138-4154.

Temple, C. (1993) *The Brain: An Introduction to the Psychology of the Human Brain and Behaviour.* London: Penguin Group.

Ten Donkelaar, H. J., Cruysberg, J. R. M., von der Vliet, T., van Domburg, P. and Renier, W. O. (2011) 'The Cranial Nerves', in ten Donkelaar, H. J. (ed.) *Clinical Neuroanatomy: Brain Circuitry and Its Disorders.* Berlin: Springer Heidelberg, pp. 249-303.

Tesink, C., Beuitelaar, J., Petersson, K., Jan van der Gaag, R., Teunisse, J. and Hagoort, P. (2011) 'Neural correlates of language comprehension in autism spectrum disorders: when language conflicts with world knowledge', *Neuropsychologia,* 49(5), pp. 1095-1104.

Thaler, H., Skewes, J. C., Gebauer, L., Christensen, P., Prkachin, K. M. and Jegindø Elmholdt, E. (2018) 'Typical pain experience but underestimation of others' pain: Emotion perception in self and others in autism spectrum disorder', *Autism* 22(6), pp. 751-762.

The Oxford English Dictionary. (2012) 'ah' Available at: https://www.oed.com/view/Entry/4264?rskey=FIrfe7&result=3&isAdvanced=false#eid (Accessed: 19 October 2019)

The Oxford English Dictionary. (1989) 'aha' Available at: http://www.oed.com/view/Entry/4265?rskey=gzWDgU&result=2#eid (Accessed: 26 September 2018)

The Oxford English Dictionary. (2008) 'boy' Available at: https://www.oed.com/view/Entry/22323?rskey=jg38xv&result=1&isAdvanced=false#eid (Accessed: 14 April 2020)

The Oxford English Dictionary. (1989) 'cognition' Available at: https://www.oed.com/view/Entry/35876?redirectedFrom=COGNITION#eid (Accessed: 04 June 2019)

The Oxford English Dictionary. (2009) 'communication' Available at: http://www.oed.com/view/Entry/37309?redirectedFrom=communication#eid (Accessed: 06 August 2018)

The Oxford English Dictionary. (2011) 'emotion' Available at: https://www.oed.com/view/Entry/61249?rskey=zm21xT&result=1&isAdvanced=false#eid (Accessed: 20 December 2019)

The Oxford English Dictionary. (2014) 'empathy' Available at: https://www.oed.com/view/Entry/61284?redirectedFrom=empathy#eid (Accessed: 21 October 2019)

The Oxford English Dictionary. (2016) 'expletive' Available at: https://www.oed.com/view/Entry/66619?redirectedFrom=expletive#eid (Accessed: 28 October 2019)

The Oxford English Dictionary. (2021) 'fear' Available at: https://www.oed.com/view/Entry/68773?rskey=KVsmkX&result=1&isAdvanced=false#eid (Accessed: 08 May 2021)

The Oxford English Dictionary. (2008) 'fuck' Available at: https://www.oed.com/view/Entry/270302?rskey=Lv5zmt&result=3&isAdvanced=false#eid (Accessed: 14 April 2020)

The Oxford English Dictionary. (2020) 'gee' Available at: https://www.oed.com/oed2/00093283 (Accessed: 14 April 2020)

The Oxford English Dictionary. (2014) 'god' Available at: https://www.oed.com/view/Entry/79625?rskey=EGrkh8&result=1&isAdvanced=false#eid (Accessed: 11 October 2019)

The Oxford English Dictionary. (1989) 'gosh' Available at: https://www.oed.com/oed2/00097084 (Accessed: 11 October 2019)

The Oxford English Dictionary. (1989) 'hey' Available at: https://www.oed.com/view/Entry/86639?rskey=U3tZCZ&result=2&isAdvanced=false#eid (Accessed: 16 April 2020)

The Oxford English Dictionary. (2013) 'irony' Available at: https://www.oed.com/view/Entry/99565?rskey=0v0BEU&result=1&isAdvanced=false#eid (Accessed: 02 August 2019)

The Oxford English Dictionary. (2008) 'language' Available at: https://www.oed.com/view/Entry/105582?rskey=5eHPDc&result=1&isAdvanced=false#eid (Accessed: 15 May 2020)

The Oxford English Dictionary. (2003) 'narrative' Available at: https://www.oed.com/view/Entry/125146?rskey=gXNNqh&result=1&isAdvanced=false#eid (Accessed: 28 May 2019)

The Oxford English Dictionary. (2019) 'oh' Available at: https://www.oed.com/view/Entry/130854?rskey=NQTMzG&result=3&isAdvanced=false#eid (Accessed: 19 October 2019)

The Oxford English Dictionary. (1989) 'oh dear' Available at: http://www.oed.com/view/Entry/47737?redirectedFrom=oh+dear#eid7273851 (Accessed: 20 October 2018)

The Oxford English Dictionary. (2021) 'oh my' Available at: https://www.oed.com/view/Entry/124420?rskey=vs5Yda&result=1&isAdvanced=false#eid35169202 (Accessed: 05 May 2021)

The Oxford English Dictionary. (2004) 'oops' Available at:
http://www.oed.com/view/Entry/131632?redirectedFrom=oops#eid (Accessed: 20 October 2018)

Collins (no date) *oops*. Available at:
https://www.collinsdictionary.com/dictionary/english/oops (Accessed: 16 April 2020)

The Oxford English Dictionary. (2004) 'ouch' Available at:
https://www.oed.com/view/Entry/133319?rskey=NRyDkR&result=2&isAdvanced=false#eid (Accessed: 28 September 2019)

The Oxford English Dictionary. (2005) 'perception' Available at:
https://www.oed.com/view/Entry/140560?redirectedFrom=PERCEPTION#eid (Accessed: 04 June 2018)

The Oxford English Dictionary. (2006) 'phonetics' Available at:
http://www.oed.com/view/Entry/142634?rskey=Qnua7h&result=2&isAdvanced=false#eid (Accessed: 20 October 2018)

The Oxford English Dictionary. (2006) 'phonology' Available at:
http://www.oed.com/view/Entry/142661?redirectedFrom=phonology#eid (Accessed: 20 October 2018)

The Oxford English Dictionary. (2021) 'pitch' Available at:
https://www.oed.com/view/Entry/144681 (Accessed: 04 April 2021)

The Oxford English Dictionary. (2008) 'sad'. Available at:
http://www.oed.com/view/Entry/169609?rskey=dAgp9R&result=2&isAdvanced=false#eid (Accessed: 05 August 2018)

The Oxford English Dictionary. (2016) 'sensation' Available at:
https://www.oed.com/view/Entry/175940?redirectedFrom=SENSATION#eid (Accessed: 04 June 2019)

The Oxford English Dictionary. (1989) 'sentence' Available at:
https://www.oed.com/view/Entry/176037?rskey=JEmnI3&result=1&isAdvanced=false#eid (Accessed: 21 July 2020)

The Oxford English Dictionary. (2011) 'shit' Available at:
https://www.oed.com/view/Entry/178330?rskey=1jkn4F&result=3&isAdvanced=false#eid (Accessed: 14 April 2020)

The Oxford English Dictionary. (1989) 'sympathy' Available at:

  http://www.oed.com/view/Entry/196271?rskey=CebJsx&result=1&isAdvanced=false#ei
  d (Accessed: 20 October 2018)

The Oxford English Dictionary. (2014) 'syntax' Available at:
  http://www.oed.com/view/Entry/196559?redirectedFrom=syntax#eid_(Accessed: 07
  August 2018)

The Oxford English Dictionary. (1989) 'ugh' Available at:

  https://www.oed.com/view/Entry/208556?redirectedFrom=ugh#eid (Accessed: 30
  September 2019)

The Oxford English Dictionary. (1989) 'uh' Available at:
  https://www.oed.com/oed2/00261373 (Accessed: 08 October 2019)

The Oxford English Dictionary. (1989) 'um' Available at:
  https://www.oed.com/oed2/00261577 (Accessed: 08 October 2019)

The Oxford English Dictionary. (1989) 'up-a-daisy' Available at:
  https://www.oed.com/oed2/00272950 (Accessed: 11 October 2019)

The Oxford English Dictionary. (1989) 'wow'. Available at:
  http://www.oed.com/view/Entry/230460?rskey=zPiFnj&result=6&isAdvanced=false#eid
  (Accessed: 28 October 2018)

The University of Chicago. (2010) *About peripheral neuropathy.* Available at:
  http://peripheralneuropathycenter.uchicago.edu/learnaboutpn/aboutpn/symptoms/threene
  rves.shtml (Accessed: 08 May 2020)

Tomblin, B. (1996) 'Genetic and environmental contributions to the risk for specific language
  impairment', in Rice, M. (ed.) *Toward a Genetics of Language.* Mahwah: Lawrence
  Erlbaum Associates, Inc, pp. 191-210.

Tomblin, B. (2011) 'Co-morbidity of autism and sli: kinds, kin and complexity',
  International Journal of Language and Communication Disorders, 46(2), pp. 127-137.

Tomblin, B. J., Hafeman, L. L. and O'Brien, M. (2003) 'Autism and autism risk in siblings of
  children with specific language impairment', *International Journal of Language and
  Communication Disorders*, 38(3), pp. 235-250.

Tseng, A., Bansal, R., Liu, J., Gerber, A. J., Goh, S., Posner, J., Colibazzi, T., Algermissen, M., Chiang, I., Russell, J. A. and Peterson, B. S. (2014) 'Using the circumplex model of affect to study valence and arousal ratings of emotional faces by children and adults with autism spectrum disorders', *Journal of Autism and Developmental Disorders*, 44(6), pp. 1332-1346.

Vernes, S. C., Newbury, D. F., Abrahams, B. S., Winchester, L., Nicod, J., Groszer, M., Alarcón, M., Oliver, P. L., Davies, K. E., Geschwind, D. H., Monaco, A. P. and Fisher, S. E. (2008) 'A functional genetic link between distinct developmental language disorders', *The New England Journal of Medicine*, 359(22), pp. 2337-2345.

Volden, J. and Lord, C. (1991) 'Neologisms and idiosyncratic language in autistic speakers', *Journal of Autism and Developmental Disorders,* 21(2), pp. 109-130.

Volden, J., Dodd, E., Engel, K., Smith, I. M., Szatmari, P., Fombonne, E., Zwaigenbaum, L., Mirenda, P., Bryson, S., Roberts, W., Vaillancourt, T., Waddell, C., Elsabbagh, M., Bennett, T., Georgiades, S. and Duku, E. (2017) 'Beyond sentences: Using the expression, reception, and recall of narratives instrument to assess communication in school-aged children with autism spectrum disorder', *Journal of Speech, Language, and Hearing Research*, 60(8), pp. 2228 – 2240.

Ward, J. (2015) *The Student's Guide to Cognitive Neuroscience*. 3rd edn. Sussex: Psychology Press.

Waxenbaum, J. A., Reddy, V. and Varacallo, M. (2020) *Anatomy, Autonomic Nervous System*. Available at: https://www.ncbi.nlm.nih.gov/books/NBK539845/ (Accessed: 24 April 2020).

Weismer, S. E. (2013) 'Developmental Language Disorders: Challenges and Implications of Cross-Group Comparisons', *Folia Phoniatrica et Logopaedica*, 65(2), pp. 68-77.

Wellman, H. M. (1992) *The Child's Theory of Mind.* United States of America: MIT Press.

Wellman, H. M. (2014) *Making Minds: How Theory of Mind Develops.* New York: Oxford University Press.

Werling, D. and Geschwind, D. (2013) 'Sex differences in autism spectrum disorders', *Current Opinion in Neurology*, 26(2), pp. 146-153.

Wetherell, D., Botting, N. and Conti-Ramsden, G. (2007) 'Narrative in adolescent specific language impairment (SLI): a comparison with peers across two different narrative genres', *International Journal of Language and Communication Disorders*, 42(5), pp. 583-605.

Wierzbicka, A. (1992) 'The semantics of interjection', *Journal of Pragmatics*, 18(2-3), pp. 159-192.

Wiig, E. H., Secord, W. and Semel, E. (1992) *Clinical Evaluation of Language Fundamentals: Preschool*. New York: The Psychological Corporation.

Wiig, E. H., Semel, E. and Secord, W. A. (2017) *Clinical Evaluation of Language Fundamentals*. 5th edn. London: Pearson Assessment.

Williams, A. (2015) *Arguments in Syntax and Semantics.* Cambridge: Cambridge University Press.

Williams, D., Botting, N. and Boucher, J. (2008) 'Language in Autism and Specific Language Impairment: What Are the Links?', *Psychological Bulletin*, 134(6), pp. 944-963.

Wharton, T. (2009) *Pragmatics and Non-Verbal Communication*. United Kingdom: Cambridge University Press.

World Health Organization. (2019) *ICD-11 for mortality and morbidity statistics. 6A02.0 Autism spectrum disorder without disorder of intellectual development and with no mild or no impairment of functional language*. Available at: https://icd.who.int/browse11/l-m/en#/http://id.who.int/icd/entity/120443468 (Accessed: 17 June 2019)

World Health Organization. (2018) *ICD-11 for mortality and morbidity statistics*. Available at: https://icd.who.int/browse11/l-m/en#/http://id.who.int/icd/entity/120443468 (Accessed: 23 August 2018)

World Health Organization. (2019) *ICD-11 for morality and morbidity statistics. 6A01.2 Developmental language disorder.* Available at: https://icd.who.int/browse11/l-m/en#/http://id.who.int/icd/entity/862918022 (Accessed: 30 October 2019)

Yiend, J., Mackintosh, B. and Savulich, G. (2012) 'Cognition and Emotion', in Braisby, N. and Gellatly, A. (ed.) *Cognitive Psychology*. 2nd edn. Oxford: Oxford University Press, pp. 508-545.